I'VE
ALWAYS
WANTED
TO.....

LEARN BASS
GUITAR

MICHELLE MARIE OSBOURNE

FOREWORD

I remember the first time meeting Michelle, and shortly after hearing her sound and feel on the bass, I knew that she not only spent time listening to other great bass players but also put the time in to master her instrument. Additionally, I saw that she is a great listener and student of music in general. I believe that Michelle has created a thorough and comprehensive tool for anyone from beginner to intermediate who wants to learn and establish a solid foundation on their instrument. From the essentials of learning the fretboard and fingering to understanding basic theory as it applies to the bass - Michelle is a consummate bass player who has the passion to inspire you to reach your full potential. Her "I've Always Wanted to Learn the Bass Guitar" eBook, I believe, will do just that.

Phil Hamilton
- Celebrity Guitarist, Guitar Coach, Composer, Educator.

ACKNOWLEDGEMENTS

Special thanks and appreciation to my family, friends, teachers, and mentors. The support and encouragement you showed during the time of writing this book kept me focused on completing this important project.

I dedicate this book to anyone seeking a little musical direction in the same way I did. I hope that the information in this book offers some sort of guidance, structure and fun to your learning so that you can pursue your musical goals in whatever way you choose!

ABOUT THIS BOOK

Do we really need another 'Learn how to play bass' study book? Well, that depends...
Everybody learns differently. We progress at different rates and have different musical goals. Whether we simply want to play for fun or play professionally, I think we can agree that we all want the freedom to express what we hear and feel whenever we pick up our instruments.

After years of playing, largely by ear, I realized that a lack of information was holding me back from reaching my musical goals. The information I received from my teachers gave me the tools that began unlocking some of these frustrations.

This book is simply a compilation of foundational music principles I've been taught along the way. Truth is, you'll find these same principles in any good music study book... but how we receive and absorb information is very much an individual thing.

That's why I have written this book with a step-by-step, clear structure in mind.

Much of this material is still a vital part of my practice routine and I'm constantly reaping the benefits of practicing the basics!

I would strongly advise you to complete each section of the book before moving on to the next chapter.

The fretboard positions and fingering options demonstrated (although comprehensive) are by no means exhaustive so I'd encourage you to explore all the possible ways you can play these scales, chords and exercises. Look out for the Study Tips as they offer some good approaches to studying the material!

To aid your learning, I have included fretboard diagrams, photos, fingering guides, bass clef notation and additional diagrams.

Example:

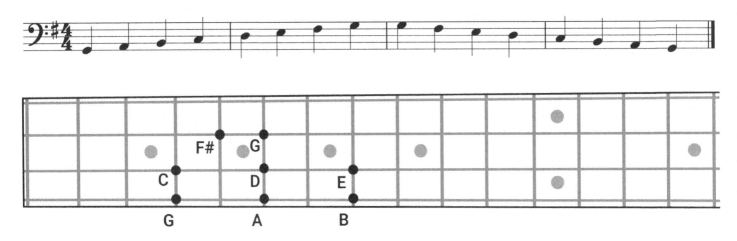

G	A	B	C	D	E	F#	G
1	2	4	1	2	4	1	2

Also available are practice play-along tracks for all the scale, triad and 7th chord exercises. These tracks are available as an additional purchase from my website. www.michellemarieosbourne.com

Let's begin!

CONTENTS

Perfect 4th 31
Perfect 5th 31
Major 6th 32
Major 7th 32
Simple Non-Diatonic Intervals 34
Minor 2nd 34
Minor 3rd 34
Augmented 4th or Tritone 35
Diminished 5th 35
Augmented 5th 36
Minor 6th 36
Minor 7th 36
Compound Intervals 37
Major 9th 38
Major 10th 38
Perfect 11th 39
Perfect 12th 39
Major 13th 39
Major 14th 40
Double Octave 40
Non-Diatonic Compound Intervals 41
Minor 9th 41
Minor 10th 41
Augmented 11th 42
Diminished 12th 42
Minor 13th 43
Inverting Intervals - 'Intervals Going Down' 44

Part 6: Triads & 7th Chords **46**
Triads 47
Major Triads 47
Minor Triads 49
Diminished Triads 51
Augmented Triads. 53
Triad Inversions 54
7th Chords 59
Major 7 59
Minor 7 61
Half-Diminished or Minor 7 ♭ 5 62

~ PART 1 ~
BASS ORIENTATION

THE ELECTRIC BASS GUITAR

The bass guitar, also known as the electric bass, has been around since the 1930s. Unlike the electric guitar, the bass guitar only has 4 strings (though 5 & 6 string basses are also common). The open string notes of the 4-string bass guitar are E A D and G.

Typically, on a 5-string bass, there is an additional low B string added. On a 6-string bass, there is an additional low B and high C string added.

In this book, all exercises have been written for a 4-string bass, but 5 and 6 string users can extend each exercise to cover the range of the bass.

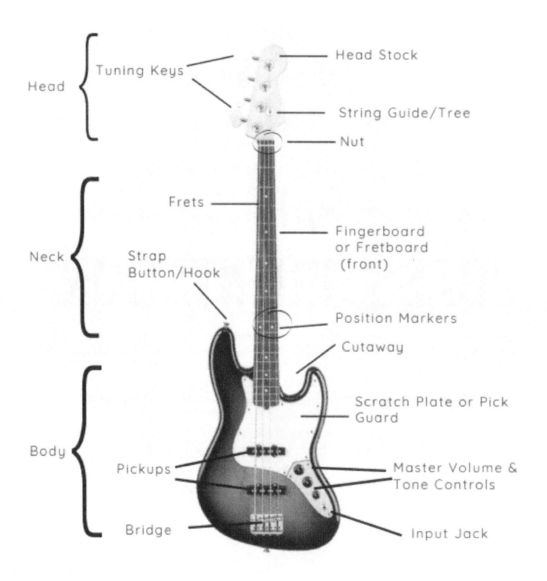

~ PART 2 ~
LEFT AND RIGHT HAND PLAYING TECHNIQUES

RIGHT HAND (PICKING HAND) TECHNIQUES

This section is designed for the complete beginner. Here we will look at the correct left and right hand playing techniques for bass guitar. I will give you a step-by-step guide on hand placement to achieve good tone and technique.

This part of the book may also prove useful for players who feel like they want to work on their tone and cross-check their current technique to determine if any adjustments need to be made.

Here we will take a look at the basic right hand (or picking hand) playing techniques. We will use the index finger, (Finger 1) to begin.

Right-handed players: place your right thumb on the pickup. If you are left-handed and play a left-handed bass, you will use the thumb of your left hand.

Exercise 1

Using the rounded tip of your index finger, play the E string by plucking the string in an upward motion, pulling the string towards you. It is important that you pluck the string towards you and not away from you in order to achieve a warmer, more rounded tone from your bass guitar.

Set your metronome to 60 bpm. Keeping your thumb on the pickup, play the first string in time with the metronome.

Play 4 beats on the E String (pluck the E string 4 times in time with the metronome). Repeat this as often as you need to before moving to the next string.

Repeat the above process on the A string, but this time, move your thumb from the pickup and place it on the E string.

By doing this, you will have better control over your picking hand when playing. Again, set yourself a task to play 4 beats on the A string. Pluck the A string 4 times in time with the metronome.

Repeat the same exercise on both the D string and the G string.

As you move to the D string, some players will feel more comfortable moving their resting thumb from the E string down to the A. Others will prefer to keep their thumb on the E string throughout.

This is a personal preference and you should go with what feels most comfortable. I encourage you to experiment with both methods and determine which works best for you. Both may feel foreign at first.

Once you are playing through these exercises comfortably, set the metronome to a higher speed of 70 bpm and repeat.

Continue to repeat this exercise, moving the metronome up by 10 bpm until you reach a target speed of 120 bpm or higher.

If increasing the speed by 10 bpm feels like a huge jump, then adjust the metronome in smaller increments of 5 bpm instead.

LEFT HAND (FRETTING HAND) TECHNIQUES

Now, let's look at the correct playing techniques for the left hand (or fretted hand).

We will use the 8th fret during this exercise as it is a good central place on the fretboard to start. The frets are slightly narrow here which will make this exercise easier to play.

Right-handed players: to start, place your left thumb on the back of the neck, behind the fretboard. Your thumb must be pointing in an upward direction (vertically) as much as possible. It will be used to support your fretted hand. This will be the other way around if you are left-handed.

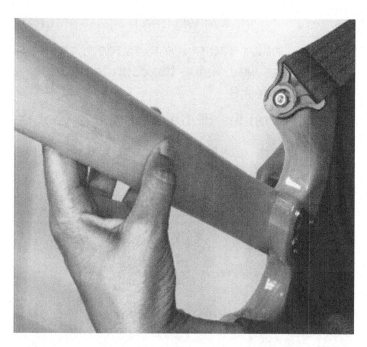

Right-handed players should take the 1st finger of their left hand and place it on the 8th fret on the fretboard. If you are left-handed, you will use the 1st finger on your right hand.

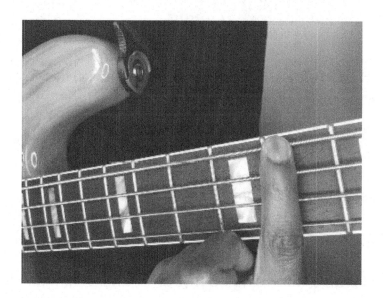

Exercise 2

Using the rounded tip of your 1st finger, press the E string firmly against the fretboard at fret 8.

The string must be pressed down fully against the fretboard to prevent it from buzzing. This is important for achieving a clean and consistent note.

Set your metronome to 60 bpm. Play the 8th fret on string E in time with the metronome. As with the previous exercises, play 4 beats on the E string. Using the picking hand techniques we've just learned, pluck the E string 4 times in time with the metronome, playing the 8th fret of each string. Repeat the above process on the A , D and G string.

1st and 2nd Finger

This time, we will introduce the 2nd finger. We will begin again at the 8th fret.

Take the 1st finger of your fretted hand and place it on the 8th fret of the fretboard, then place your 2nd finger on fret 9. In the same way, using the rounded tip of your 2nd finger, firmly press the E string against the fretboard at fret 9.

Remember to keep your 1st finger on the 8th fret and to use your thumb to support your left hand.

Exercise 3

Set your metronome to 60 bpm. Play fret 8 with your 1st finger on the first beat of the metronome. Then, using your 2nd finger, play fret 9 on the second beat of the metronome.

On the 3rd beat of the metronome, go back to playing fret 8 with your 1st finger and on the 4th beat, play fret 9 again with your 2nd finger. Here we are essentially alternating between both fingers.

Keep playing this exercise until you become comfortable using both fingers on your fretted hand.

3rd and 4th Finger

Once you become comfortable with using both your 1st and 2nd finger, slowly introduce your 3rd and 4th finger.

With your 1st finger on the 8th fret, place your 2nd finger on fret 9, your 3rd finger on fret 10, and your 4th finger on fret 11. All four fingers should be covering the span of all 4 frets.

This fretted hand technique is known as the "finger per fret rule". As bass players. it is important to become comfortable using this technique as it will allow for the development of speed and accuracy as you begin to play more complicated bass lines.

Exercise 4

Setting the metronome to 60 bpm again. Play each fret one at a time using the finger per fret technique. Repeat the above process on the A string, D string and G string, starting on the 8th fret of each string every time.

Now that you are beginning to get used to playing finger per fret exercises on your left hand, let's play through the next series of fretted hand exercises.

With your 1st finger on fret 8 (note C), play through the following finger exercises. Use the fretboard diagram and the fingering tables below as a guide. The top row of the fingering table represents the finger you should be using and the bottom row represents the note you should be playing.

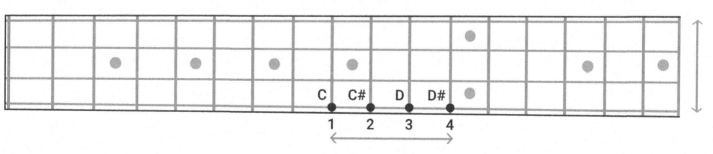

Exercise 5 - 1234 4321

Fingering Table

1	2	3	4	4	3	2	1
C	C#	D	D#	D#	D	C#	C

Exercise 6-1324

1	3	2	4	1	3	2	4
C	D	C#	D#	C	D	C#	D#

Exercise 7- 4231

4	2	3	1	4	2	3	1
D#	C#	D	C	D#	C#	D	C

You can move these exercises around to start at different areas on the fretboard. Remember to increase the speed of the metronome as you become comfortable with each exercise.

It's important to note that although the finger per fret technique is an important one, it isn't always the best approach to use. Keep this in mind whenever you are learning a bass line or groove.

MUTED TECHNIQUE

A popular technique used in bass playing is the muted technique. Although this chapter is designed to only focus on the basics of playing techniques, I found it necessary to include the muted playing technique.

You may see and hear this technique being used in genres like Reggae, Jazz, Gospel and Blues music, but essentially, there is no rule on when and where this muted technique should be used.

To begin, place the palm of your right-hand across the strings over the pickups. Apply just enough pressure to restrict any sound coming from the strings. Use your left hand if you are left-handed and play a left-handed bass.

The goal is to ensure that your palm is muting the strings you want to play. Using the width of your hand, you will probably be able to mute 2 to 3 strings at once. Try to achieve this if possible.

Using your right-hand thumb and with your palm resting against the strings, try playing a series of notes with your thumb moving in a downwards direction against the string. Starting on the E string, play 4 notes. Then, move through the A, D and G string in the same way, playing 4 notes on each string. When you feel comfortable, introduce the metronome to this exercise.

When you start to become comfortable with the muted thumb exercise, begin to introduce your 1st finger on your right hand.

Alternate between your thumb and 1st finger. Your 1st finger should move in an upward direction against the string. Again, begin on the E string and play 4 notes on each string. For those playing a left-handed bass, you will be using your left hand to play this technique.

You can extend your muted technique practice by playing through the previous left-hand exercises (Exercise 5-7). Remember to always play along with the metronome when practicing this muted bass technique.

~ PART 3 ~
AN INTRODUCTION TO MUSIC THEORY

THE 12 MUSICAL NOTES

Typically, 12 musical notes exist in modern western music. These 12 notes are all different in terms of pitch (sound). We use the first seven letters of the alphabet and a combination of symbols called sharps (#) and flats (♭) to name these notes.

Some of these notes are given more than one name, as described in music as an enharmonic equivalent. Although these notes have alternative names, there are only 12 notes (in terms of pitch) that exist in total.

The table below displays these 12 notes and their enharmonic equivalent names. The 12 notes can also be described as the chromatic scale.

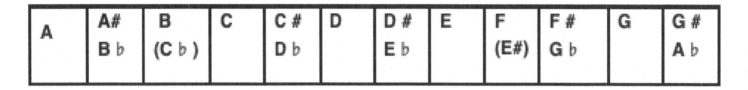

A few things to take note of:

These notes will either be listed as a natural note (♮) a sharp note (#) or a flat (♭) note. If we take a look at the makeup of a piano, we can see that the natural notes fall on the white keys and the sharp and flat notes fall on the black keys.

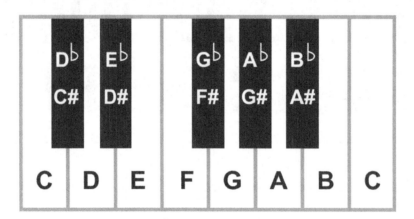

You may have noticed that I have put note C ♭ and E # in brackets on the previous table and that they are not labeled on the piano diagram. This is because there will be occurrences in music where we will need to change the name of note B to a C ♭ and note F to an E #, therefore it is important to mention here. This will become clearer as we begin to understand the rules of the major scale. We will explore this later on in the book.

NOTES ACROSS THE FRETBOARD

Now that we know the 12 musical notes, we will begin the process of memorizing these musical notes across the fretboard. We will look at each note, string by string, and will use a combination of string plus fret number to memorize the note names.

Note: This has been written for a 4 string, 24 fret bass.

Taking one note at a time, start to memorize each note by location.

Study Tip! 💡

Don't try to submit it to memory all at once. Learn one or two notes per week. Only move on when you are confident that you know it by heart.

FRET 1 – 12

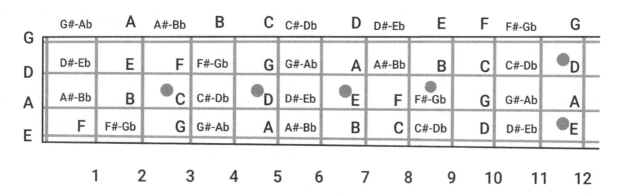

FRET 13 – 24

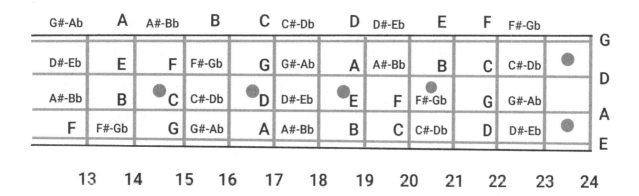

15

FRETBOARD LOCATION TABLES

Note A

String Name	Fret Number
E	5 & 17
A	Open, 12 & 24
D	7 & 19
G	2 & 14

Note A# - Bb

String Name	Fret Number
E	6 & 18
A	1 & 13
D	8 & 20
G	3 & 15

Note B

String Name	Fret Number
E	7 & 19
A	2 & 14
D	9 & 21
G	4 & 16

Note C

String Name	Fret Number
E	8 & 20
A	3 & 15
D	10 & 22
G	5 & 17

Note C# - Db

String Name	Fret Number
E	9 & 21
A	4 & 16
D	11 & 23
G	6 & 18

Note D

String Name	Fret Number
E	10 & 22
A	5 & 17
D	Open, 12 & 24
G	7 & 19

Note D# - Eb

String Name	Fret Number
E	11 & 23
A	6 & 18
D	1 & 13
G	8 & 20

Note E

String Name	Fret Number
E	Open, 12 & 24
A	7 & 19
D	2 & 14
G	9 & 21

Note F

String Name	Fret Number
E	1 & 13
A	8 & 20
D	3 & 15
G	10 & 22

Note F# - Gb

String Name	Fret Number
E	2 & 14
A	9 & 21
D	4 & 16
G	11 & 23

Note G

String Name	Fret Number
E	3 & 15
A	10 & 22
D	5 & 17
G	Open, 12 & 24

Note G# - Ab

String Name	Fret Number
E	4 & 16
A	11 & 23
D	6 & 18
G	1 & 13

SEMITONE SHAPES ACROSS THE FRETBOARD

Here's a look at what semitones look like on the fretboard of a bass guitar using notes A and Bb as an example.

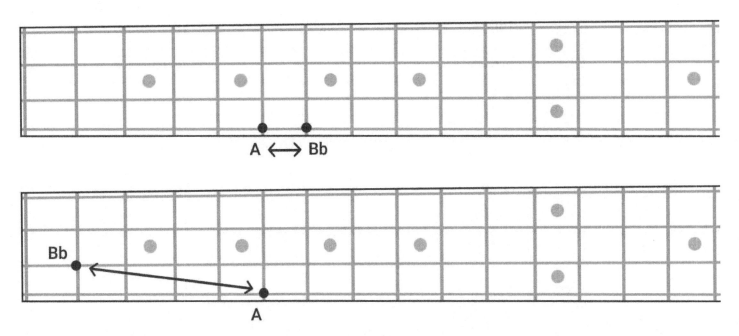

TONE SHAPES ACROSS THE FRETBOARD

Here's what a tone shape looks like on the fretboard of a bass guitar. I have used notes A and B as an example.

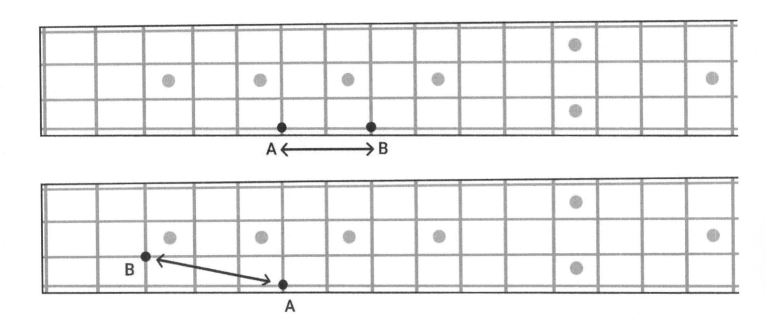

AN INTRODUCTION TO THE MAJOR SCALE

The major scale is one of the most common scales used in modern western music. Like all other scales, it derives from the 12 music notes.

We create the major scale using a combination of intervals called whole- tones (also known as tones) and semitones. In music, an interval is simply the distance between two notes.

In this section, we will only be looking at two intervals: tones and semitones.

We will look further into the other intervals later on in the book.

If you refer back to the 12 musical notes, a semitone is the movement (either up or down) of one note or one fret. i.e. A to A # or E to F.

A tone is the movement (either up or down) of two notes or two frets.

i.e. A to B or E to F#. Refer to the fretboard diagram to visualize these examples.

THE MAJOR SCALE FORMULA

Below is the combination of tones and semitones used to create the major scale.

Tone Tone Semitone Tone Tone Tone Semitone or often written in short as T T S T T T S.

Here are some important rules to know when writing the notes of the major scale.

Some keys are considered flat (♭) keys and some are considered sharp (#) keys, therefore we should never name sharps and flats in the same key.

Never repeat the same letter name twice when writing the major scale, i.e. A and A #. Here you would need to use B ♭ instead of A #. The Circle of Fifths section of the book looks at this concept in a little more detail.

Now that we have covered some of the basic rules of the major scale, work out the notes of all 12 major scale keys using the scale formula.

A	A# B♭	B (C♭)	C	C # D♭	D	D # E♭	E	F (E#)	F # G♭	G	G # A♭

Study Tip!

As I mentioned before, it is always best to learn little and often. Take one scale per week, and together with the scale positions learn the notes in the scale. Just think, in 12 weeks you will memorize all the notes of the major scale keys and will be well on your way to playing them, knowing them over the entire fretboard.

Only move on when you are confident that you know it completely.

~ PART 4 ~
THE MAJOR SCALE AND THE FRETBOARD

Now that we are familiar with how the major scale is built up, lets learn to play it across the fretboard. We will begin with playing the shapes over one octave.

An octave is the interval measurement of 12 semitones. So if we play note 'G' and count 12 semitones up, we will land on a higher-pitched 'G'.

This is also the case if we count 12 semitones down. If we are counting using the steps of the major scale, an octave will be eight diatonic notes away from its starting note.

G- A - B - C - D - E - F# - G

In short, an octave it is the same note with double the pitch going up or half the pitch going down. The following major scale shapes are shown in the Key of G.

Study Tip!

As with every exercise, once you get used to the shapes, play the scale in all 12 keys. This will ensure that you will become familiar with playing in every key across the entire fretboard.

Naming the notes of the scale is also essential so that you begin to submit the notes to memory. This will also help reinforce their location on the fretboard.

MAJOR SCALE SHAPE ACROSS THE FRETBOARD

Play through the following scale using your first finger.

Exercise 8 - G Major Scale

G Major Scale - Across 1 string

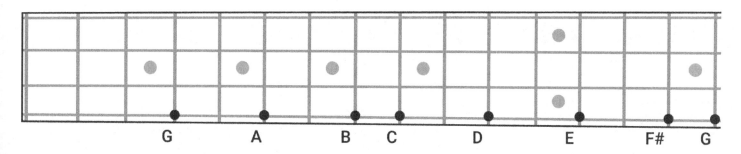

Exercise 9 - G Major Scale - Across 2 Strings

Here we use the 'finger per fret rule'. This is important as we want to be able to move through each note as smoothly as possible.

In this section, I have included a table that will give you a 'fingering guide' to use when playing through these scale patterns. The number below each note is the finger you should use to play that particular note.

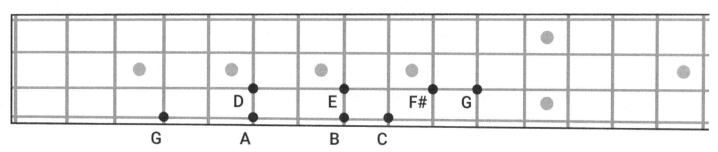

Fingering Table

G	A	B	C	D	E	F#	G
1	1	3	4	1	1	3	4

Exercise 10 - G Major Scale - Across Three Strings

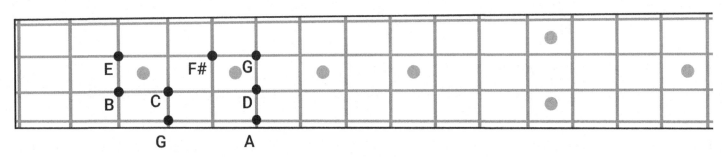

G	A	B	C	D	E	F#	G
1	2	4	1	2	4	1	2

Option 2

G	A	B	C	D	E	F#	G
2	4	1	2	4	1	3	4

Exercise 11 - G Major Scale - Across Four Strings

G	A	B	C	D	E	F#	G
4	1	3	4	1	3	1	2

Exercise 12 - G Major Scale - Across Two Octaves

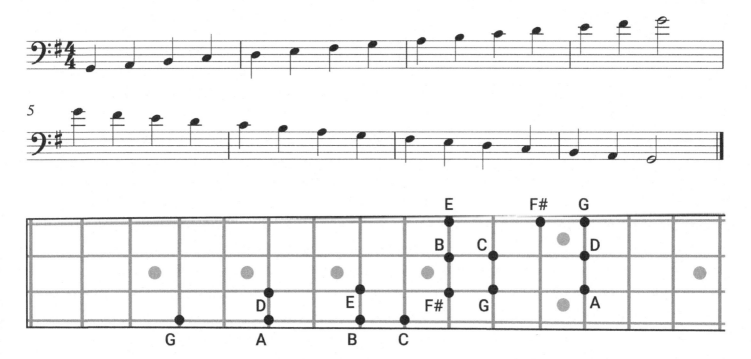

1st Octave

G	A	B	C	D	E	F#
1	1	3	4	1	1	3

2nd Octave

G	A	B	C	D	E	F#	G
4	4	1	2	4	1	3	4

Study Tip! ☀️

There are several ways you can play the major scale over two octaves. Using a combination of the examples you have been shown, see how many other ways you can play this scale over two octaves.

In all examples, learn to play the scale both ascending and descending. Remember to play them with a metronome and challenge yourself to play them at higher speeds.

CAGED SYSTEM

We must be able to play all scales across the entire 4 string span before we shift our hand position. This means we should continue playing the scale in that same position until we reach the last possible note on the last string before shifting. We may not necessarily be able to complete the scale, but we must be aware of the last possible note we can play. This approach is known as the CAGED approach.

The fretboard diagram below shows an example of the G major scale played using this 'CAGED' system of playing scales. The goal is to use this approach with every scale and chord we learn to play.

Exercise 13 - G Major Scale - CAGED

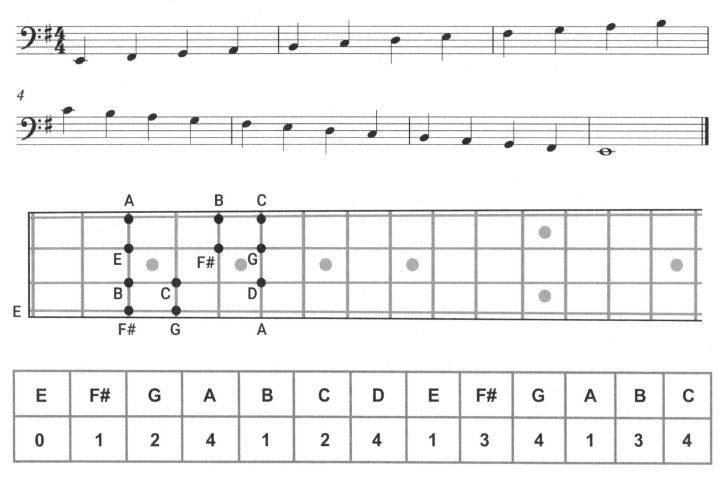

E	F#	G	A	B	C	D	E	F#	G	A	B	C
0	1	2	4	1	2	4	1	3	4	1	3	4

~ PART 5 ~
INTERVALS

INTERVAL TABLE - SIMPLE INTERVALS

As mentioned earlier in Part 3, an interval is the distance between two notes. This distance is measured using semitones. When counting, we include both the starting and the ending note. The table below outlines how many semitones equal each interval.

INTERVAL NAME	SEMITONES
UNISON	0
MINOR 2ND	1
MAJOR 2ND	2
MINOR 3RD	3
MAJOR 3RD	4
PERFECT 4TH	5
TRITONE	6
PERFECT 5TH	7
MINOR 6TH	8
MAJOR 6TH	9
MINOR 7TH	10
MAJOR 7TH	11
OCTAVE	12

Intervals can be categorized as Simple or Compound. A simple interval is an interval that falls within the octave of a scale.

Intervals can also be categorized as Diatonic or Non-diatonic/Chromatic Intervals.

A diatonic interval is one that falls within the scale. For example, in the G major scale, the distance between notes G and A will be described as a diatonic interval, as A is one of the notes within the G major scale.

The distance between notes G and A# however would be considered a non-diatonic interval as A# is outside the G major scale.

In this section, we will learn the name and shapes of each interval across the fretboard. We will look at this using examples of intervals going 'up'.

Play through each of the following intervals and start to memorize the shape of each interval.

We will start with the intervals of the major scale. Each interval will either be a Major or a Perfect Interval. Major and Perfect are terms used to define the quality of the note within the context of the scale.

SIMPLE DIATONIC INTERVALS

Unison

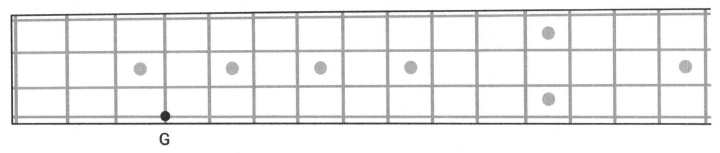

G

Major 2nd

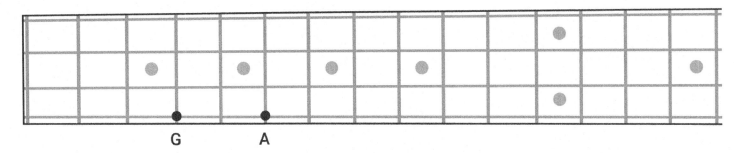

G   A

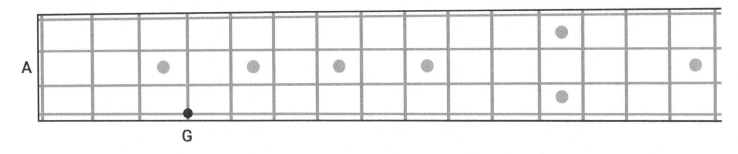

A

G

Major 3rd

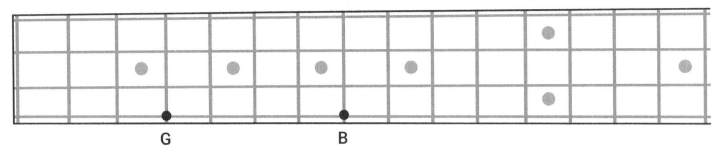

G   B

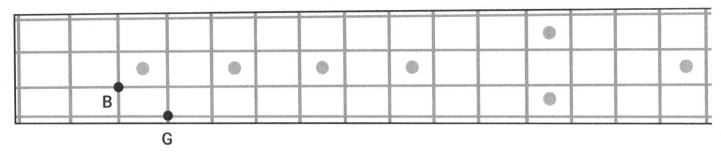

B

G

PERFECT INTERVALS

A fourth and fifth is known as perfect because its pitch carries less tension or dissonance when being played than the other intervals.

For example, a major third interval has the ability to completely change the quality of a chord and that change is much more noticeable to our ears than that of a perfect fourth or fifth.

Unison and octave intervals are also known as perfect intervals.

Perfect 4th

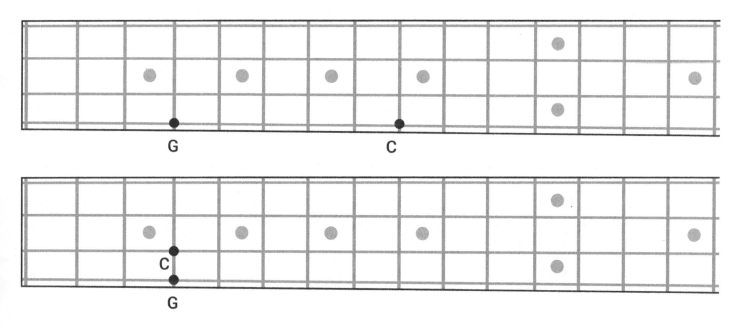

Perfect 5th

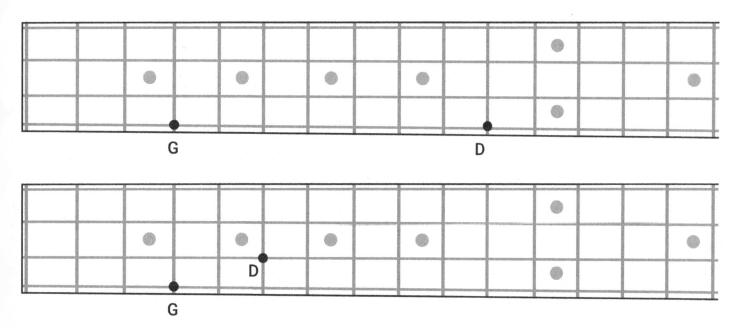

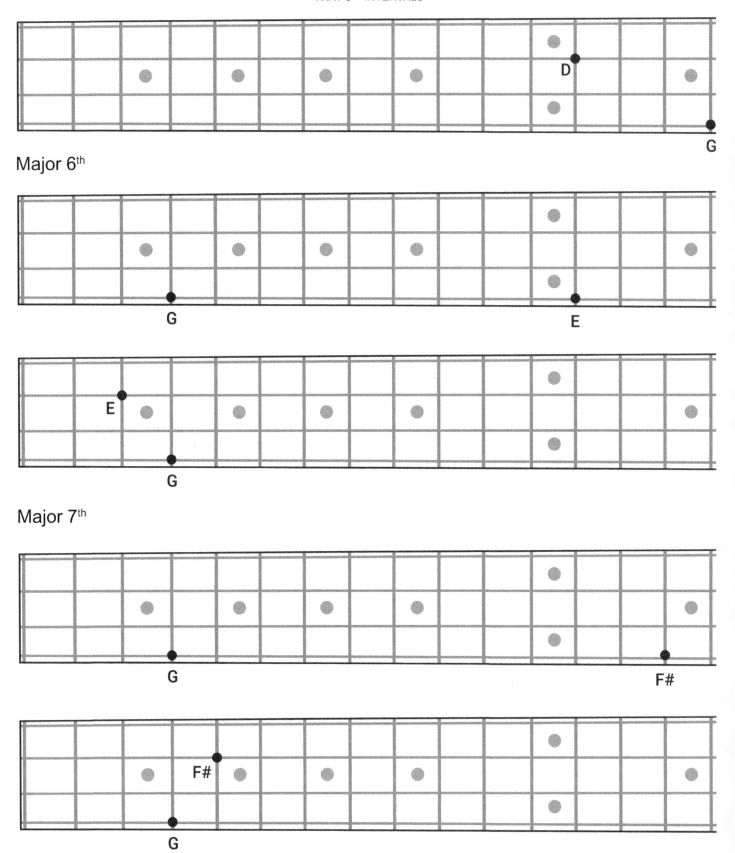

Major 6th

Major 7th

Octave

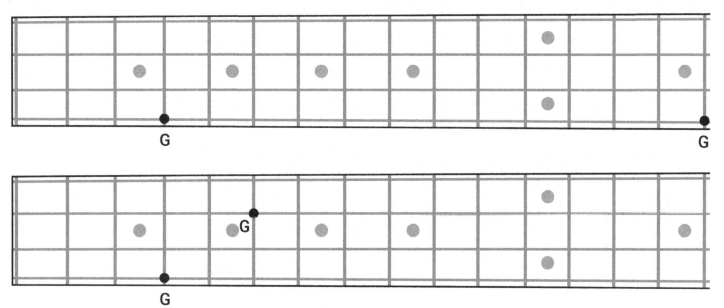

G   G

G

G

SIMPLE NON-DIATONIC INTERVALS

Now, let's take a look at the non-diatonic interval shapes.

If diatonic intervals fall within the major scale, then the non-diatonic intervals are the remaining notes that we didn't play in between.

So, using the G major scale as an example, the notes outside of the scale will be:

G #/ A ♭ , A #/ B ♭ , C # / D ♭ , D #/ E ♭ and F

As we are learning non-diatonic intervals, each interval can either be named a minor, diminished, or augmented interval. Again, these terms define the quality of the note within the context of the key.

Here are a few things to know:

A 2nd, 3rd, 6th and 7th interval can be major or minor.

A 4th, 5th, 8th and unison interval can be diminished, augmented and perfect.

Here are the names and shapes of these non-diatonic intervals.

Minor 2nd

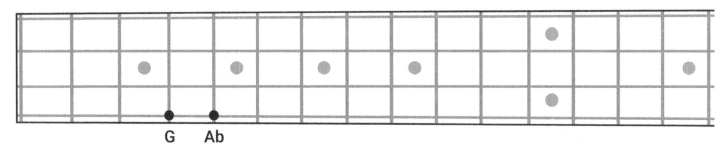

G   Ab

Minor 3rd

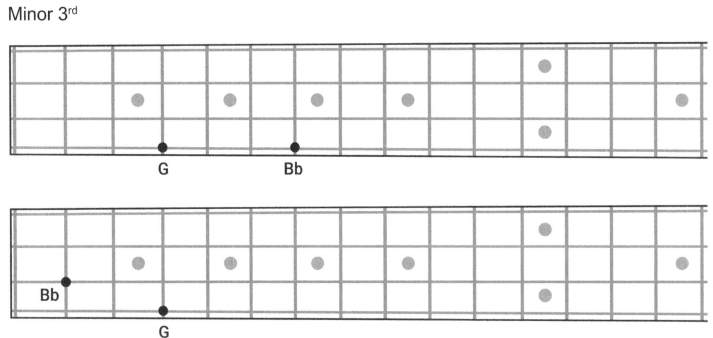

G   Bb

Bb

G

Augmented 4th or Tritone

An Augmented 4th is the same note in terms of pitch as the Diminished 5th. Here are the fretboard shapes.

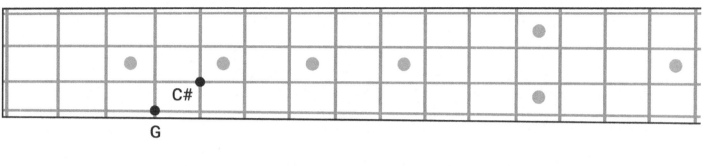

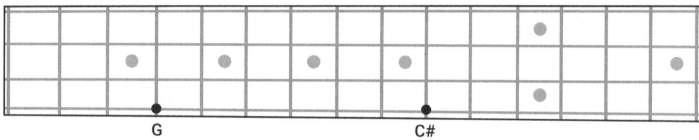

Diminished 5th

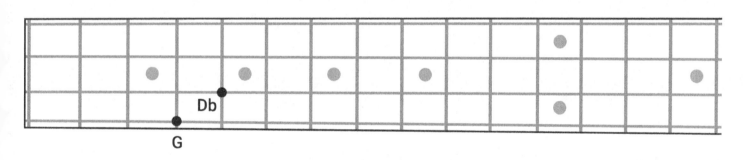

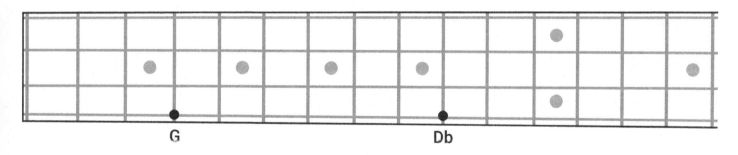

Augmented 5th

An Augmented 5th is the same note in terms of pitch as the Minor 6th. Here are the fretboard shapes.

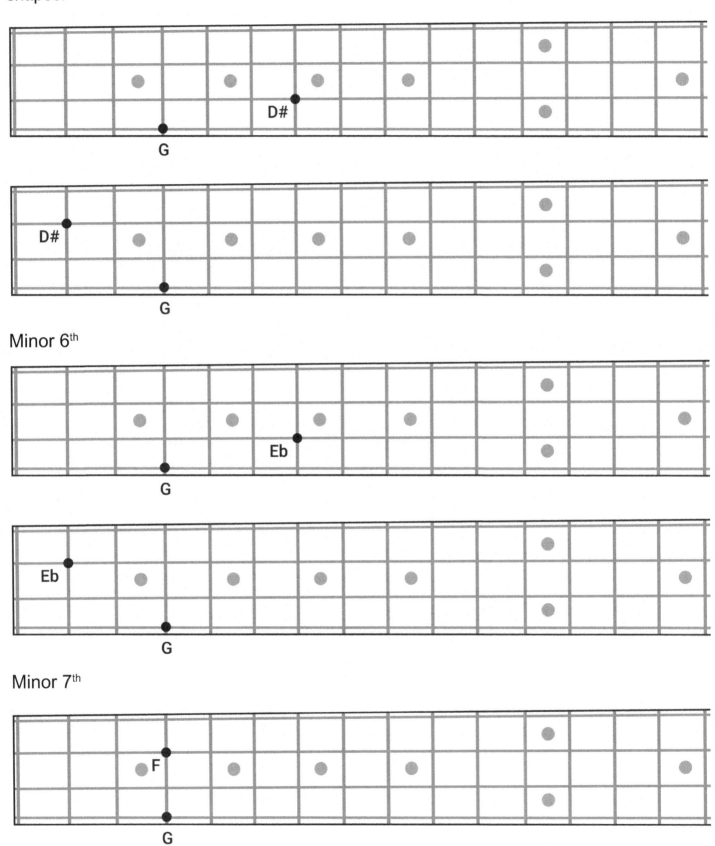

Minor 6th

Minor 7th

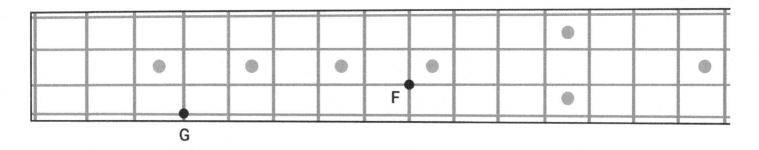

COMPOUND INTERVALS

A compound interval is an interval that extends beyond the octave of a scale. We continue to follow the major scale formula and keep counting. Compound intervals follow the same rules as simple intervals.

INTERVAL NAME	SEMITONES
MINOR 9TH	13
MAJOR 9TH	14
MINOR 10TH	15
MAJOR 10TH	16
PERFECT 11TH	17
AUGMENTED 11TH	18
PERFECT 12TH	19
MINOR 13TH	20
MAJOR 13TH	21
MINOR 14TH	22
MAJOR 14TH	23
DOUBLE OCTAVE	24

Using the G major scale, the next note in the scale after the octave will be an A but its interval will be called a 9th. The following note B will be a 10th and so on. The table below outlines how many semitones equal each compound interval.

Staying in the key of G, here are what these compound interval shapes look like on the fretboard. We'll start with the diatonic intervals.

Major 9th

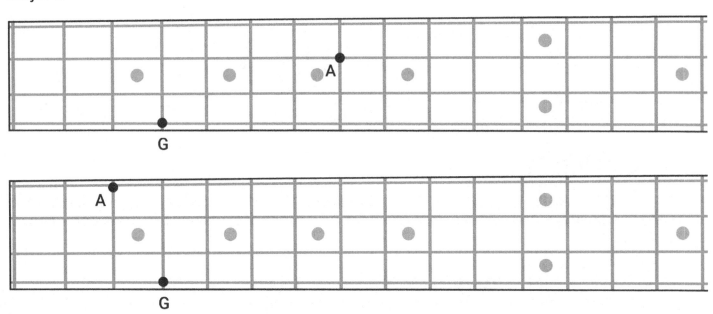

Major 10th

Although numerically correct, in the context of a chord, a 10th interval is commonly referred to as a 3rd. The 3rd (depending on the chord quality) already appears in a structure of a chord and plays an important role in defining the chord. So, in the context of chord extensions, a 10th would not be named in the chord. This is also the case when the 10th interval is modified to a minor interval.

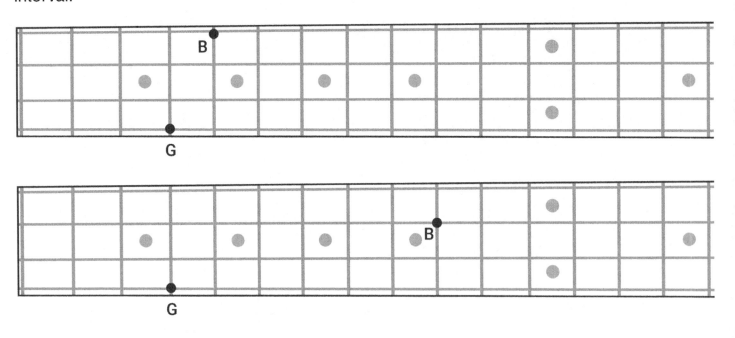

Perfect 11th

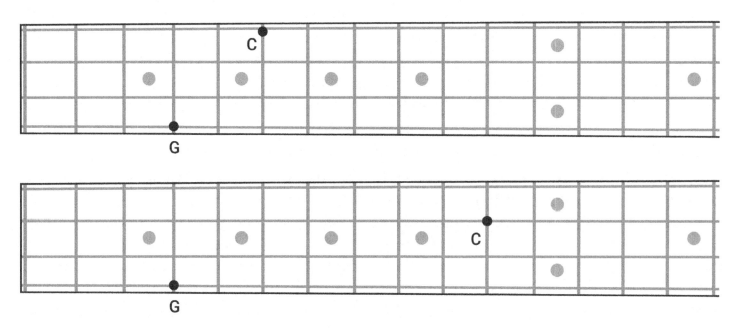

Perfect 12th

As with the 10th interval, the 12th interval is referred to as a 5th. Again this is the case when the 12th interval is modified to a diminished or augmented interval.

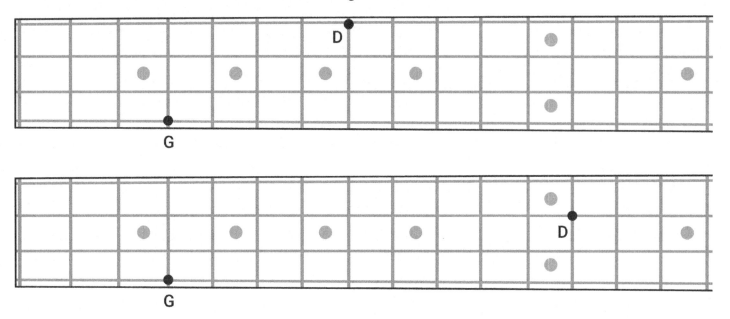

Major 13th

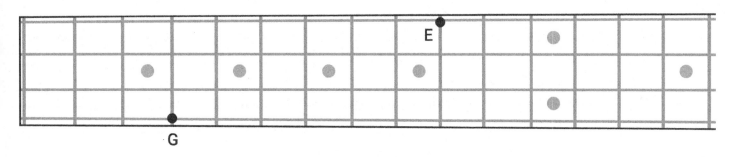

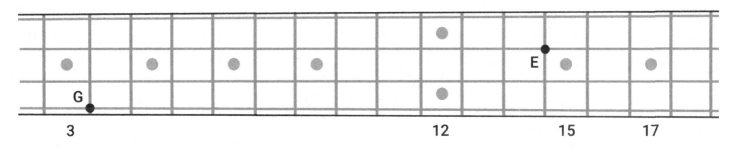

Major 14th

As with the 10 and 12th interval, the 14th interval is referred to as a 7th. Again, this is the case when the 14th interval is modified to a minor interval.

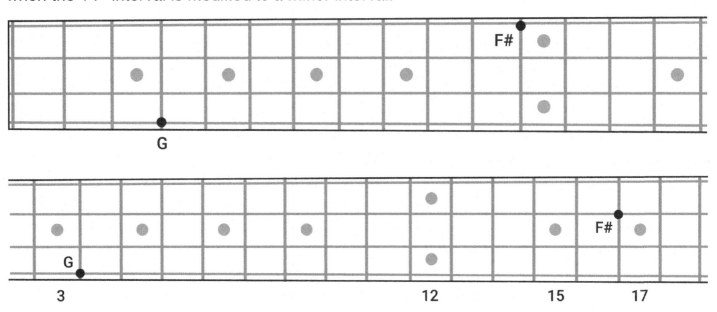

Double Octave

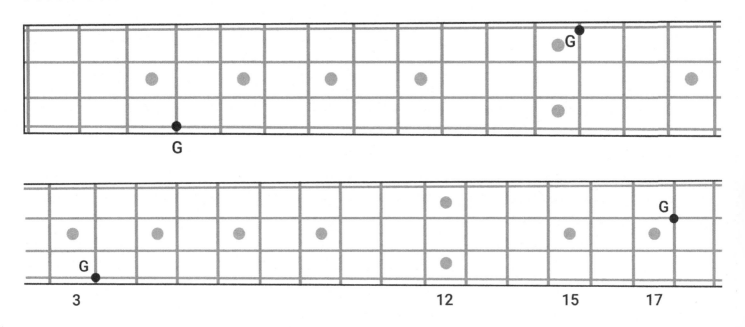

NON-DIATONIC COMPOUND INTERVALS

Just like the diatonic compound intervals, the varied 10th, 12th and 14th intervals are not named as such since they will have previously been named as 3rds, 5ths and 7ths (of some variation) within the context of the chord structure.

Minor 9th

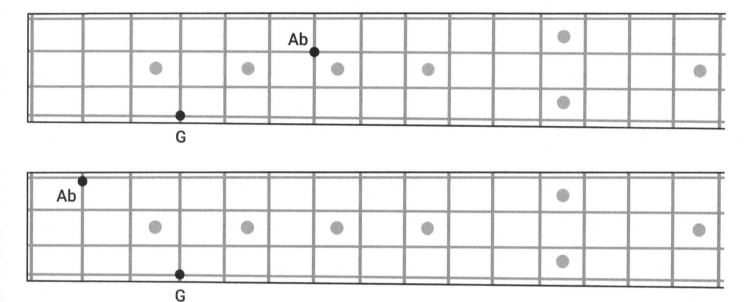

Minor 10th

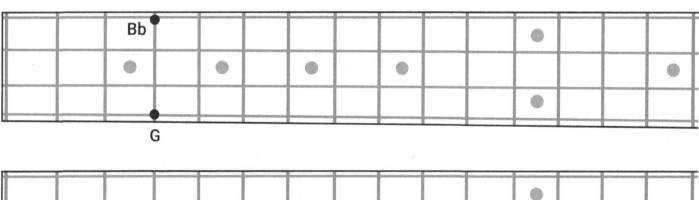

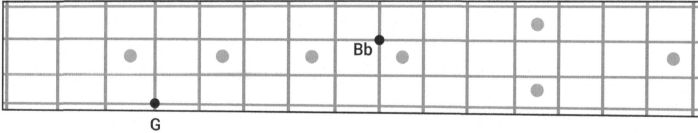

Augmented 11th

Just like its simple interval equivalent, an Augmented 11 is the same note in terms of pitch as the Diminished 12th. Here are the fretboard shapes.

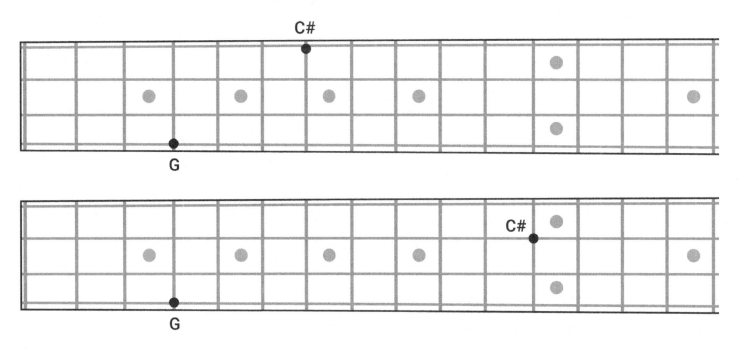

Diminished 12th

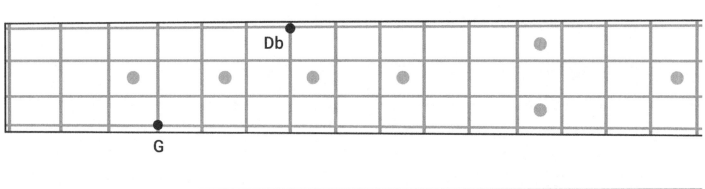

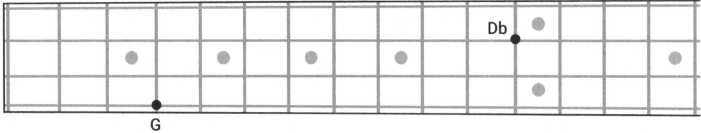

Minor 13th

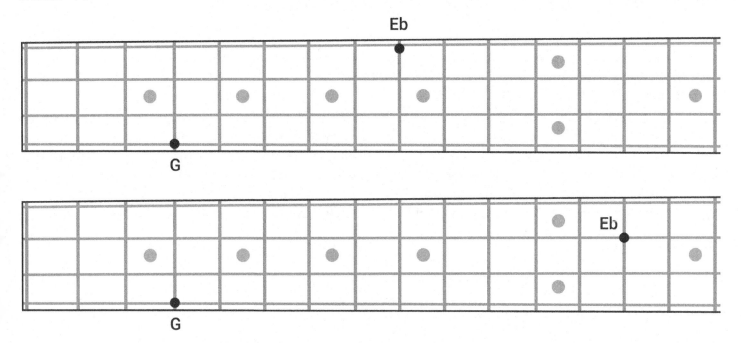

Although most of the interval shapes are covered here, there are some others as well. Take the time to find all of the shapes across the fretboard and as always move the shapes around in all 12 keys.

INVERTING INTERVALS - 'INTERVALS GOING DOWN'

So far, all the intervals we have looked at have been intervals going 'up', or in other words, intervals played above the root note or tonic. If we were to play the same interval below the root note, that note would be different. Remember, this is because we measure intervals using semitones. Let's take a look at the following.

Diagram 1 shows an example of a major 2nd interval going up. As we've learned, a major 2nd interval equals 2 semitones, but when we count 2 semitones going down, we arrive on a completely different note (see Diagram 2). Therefore, if we were to play note 'A' below our starting note 'G', the correct interval would be a minor 7 as we would have to count the distance of 10 semitones before we would arrive at note 'A' (see Diagram 3). I have added note 'G' on the E string in Diagram 3 so that it is easier to visually see the measurement of 10 semitones.

Diagram 1

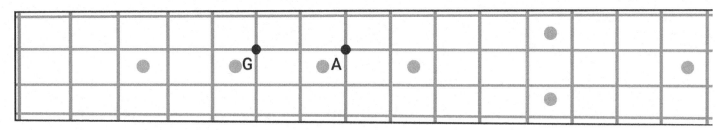

Diagram 2

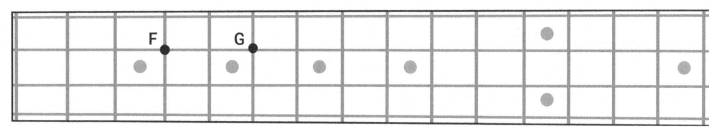

Diagram 3

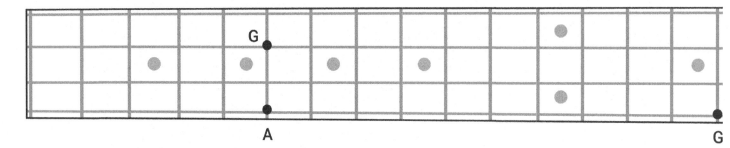

Here are some points that will help you to remember the principles of measuring intervals going down.

1. A major interval going up will invert to a minor interval going down and vice versa.
2. A diminished interval going up will invert to an augmented interval going down and vice versa.
3. Numerically, if you subtract the interval number from the number 9, it will give you the inverted interval. i.e. referencing the previous example, the interval of a 2nd will invert to an interval of a 7th. 9 minus 2 equals 7.

The table below will help as a reference point for inverting intervals.

CHORD QUALITY	
MAJOR	MINOR
MINOR	MAJOR
PERFECT	PERFECT
DIMINISHED	AUGMENTED
AUGMENTED	DIMINISHED
INTERVAL NUMBER	
UNISON	UNISON
2ND	7TH
3RD	6TH
4TH	5TH
5TH	4TH
6TH	3RD
7TH	2ND
OCTAVE	OCTAVE

~ PART 6 ~
TRIADS & 7th CHORDS

TRIADS

Triads are simply 3 note chords which are created from scales. They play a huge part in music and are an essential part of learning to play any instrument and song. It is vitally important that we learn all triad types across the entire fretboard.

The 4 main triad types are Major, Minor, Diminished and Augmented, and are made up of a combination of both Major and Minor 3rd intervals. The previous work done on intervals will be very important to understanding chords and triads, so you must have a firm understanding of intervals before moving on to learning triads.

Let's take a look at each triad type starting with the Major triad.

MAJOR TRIADS

To create a major triad, we simply take the 1st, 3rd and 5th note of the major scale. Using the 'A' major scale as an example, A - B- C# - D- E- F# - G# - A, the 1st, 3rd & 5th notes would be A, C# & E.

If we take a closer look, we can see that the distance from note A to C# is an interval of a major 3rd and C# to E is an interval of a minor 3rd. Therefore, a major triad is constructed by playing a major 3rd interval followed by a minor 3rd interval.

Here are the major triad shapes across 1, 2 and 3 strings. As bass players, we must learn them in all positions. Play through each shape.

Study Tip

When you become comfortable, add the octave to the triad and play A, C# E & A.

Then, play each triad shape in reverse and, as always, ensure that you are playing along with the metronome.

A Major Triad

Exercise 14

A Major Triad – Across 1 String

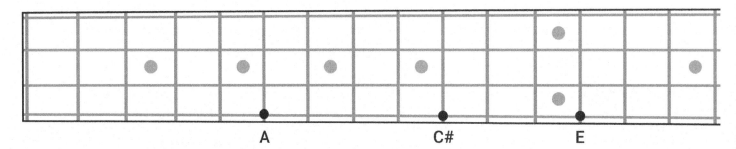

A Major Triad – Across 2 Strings

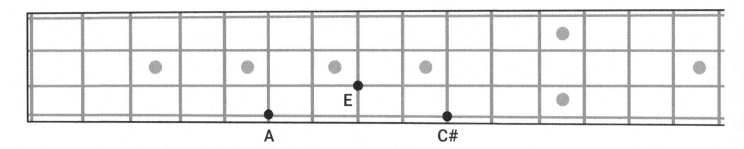

Option 2

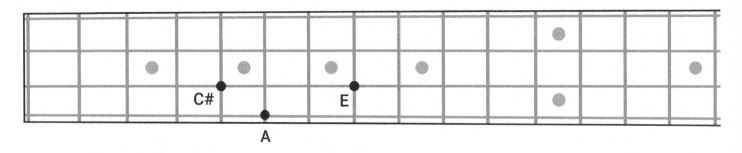

A Major Triad – Across 3 Strings

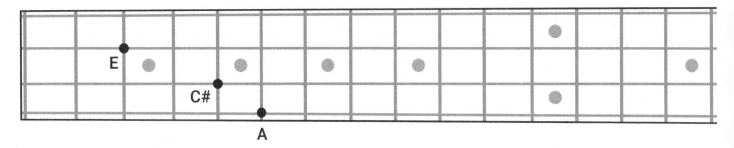

MINOR TRIADS

A minor triad is similar to the major triad, but this time move the major 3rd interval down by 1 semitone to make a minor 3rd interval. We simply flatten the 3rd. A minor triad is therefore made up of a minor 3rd interval followed by a major 3rd interval. The notes would be A, C & E.

A Minor Triad

Exercise 15

A Minor Triad – Across 1 String

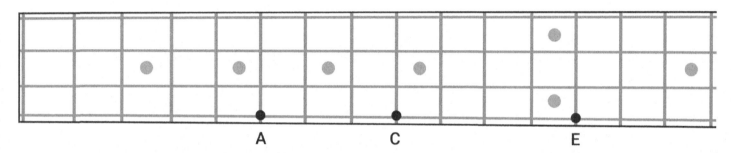

A Minor Triad – Across 2 Strings

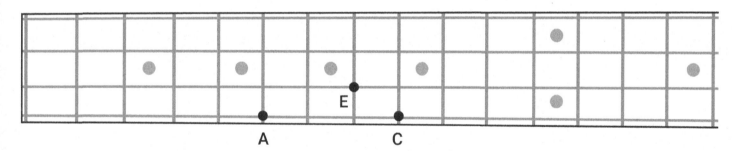

Option 2

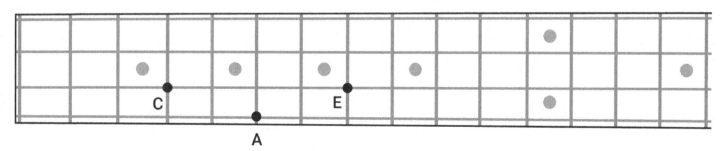

A Minor Triad – Across 3 Strings

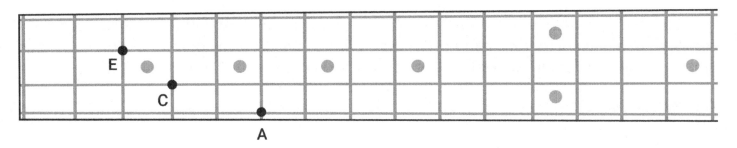

DIMINISHED TRIADS

Similar to the minor triad, the diminished triad has a minor (or flattened 3rd) but also has a diminished 5th (or flattened 5th) interval. This means the perfect 5th interval moves down a semitone to create the flattened 5th or tritone interval. The notes in the A diminished triad are A, C & E♭.

A Diminished Triad

Exercise 16

A Diminished Triad - Across String 1

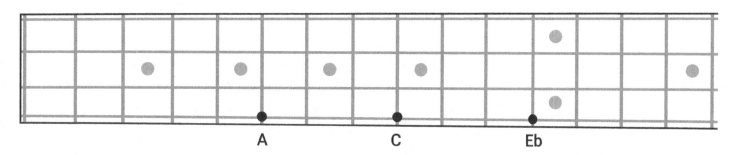

A Diminished Triad - Across String 2

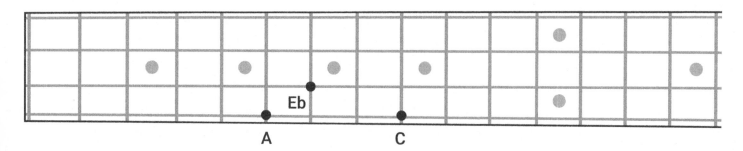

Option 2

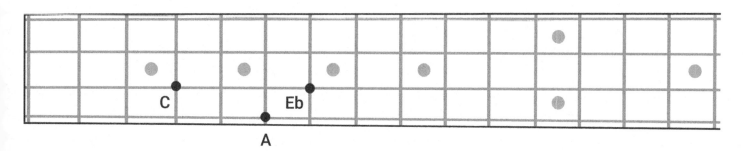

A Diminished Triad Across String 3

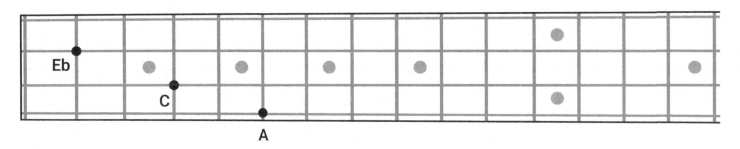

AUGMENTED TRIADS

An Augmented triad is made up of a major 3rd interval followed by another major 3rd interval. The notes in the A Augmented triad are A, C# & E# (E# is the enharmonic name for F. In Part 3 of the book we talked about the enharmonic names which are notes that have the same pitch but different names.)

As we are referring to a 5th interval, it will be an E (of some sort), as note E is the 5th interval of the A major scale. It cannot be an F as 1) F has already been used in the A major scale as a 6th interval and 2) we cannot use the same letter name twice.

For the same reasons, a diminished 5th interval in the key of A major would be a E♭ and not a D#.

Below are the examples of the Augmented triad across the fretboard.

A Augmented Triad
Exercise 17

A Augmented Triad Across 1 String

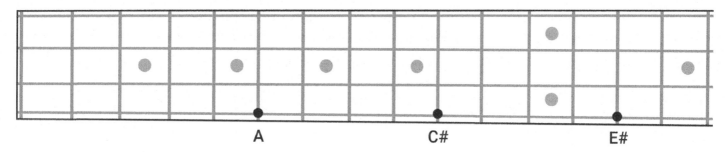

A Augmented Triad - Across 2 string

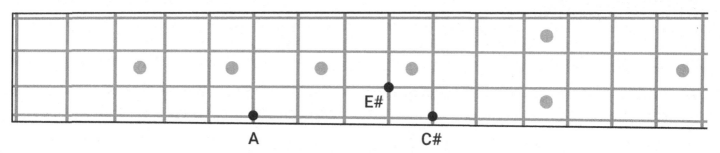

Option 2

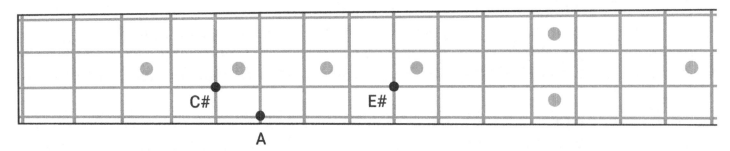

A Augmented Triad Across 3 Strings

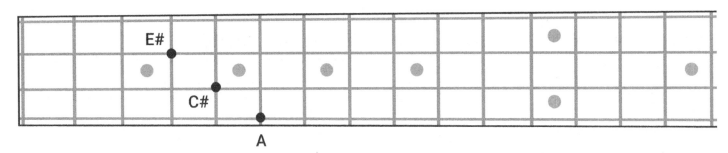

Study Tip

Take the time to familiarize yourself with both the shape of each triad and the note names of each triad. Do this for all 12 keys.

Remember, if you have taken the time to recite the notes in the major scale, remembering the notes of the triad will come a lot quicker and easier. If need be, go back to Part 4 of the book and spend some time submitting these notes to your muscle memory.

Once you feel confident playing each triad shape, start to play them as inversions. For example, instead of playing an 'A' major triad as A, C# E and back to A, start on the 3rd, C# and play C#, E, A then back to C#.

TRIAD INVERSIONS

Playing triads as inversions are vital for improvising, creating basslines and playing chords, so don't skip this important step in the learning process.

I've included an example of what the Major, Minor, Diminished and Augmented triad inversions look like. Take the time to work out the inversions using all string options.

I want to encourage you to work out the inversion shapes based on the information we have learned in this chapter. The work we do here will prove vital later on down the road.

A Major Triad Inversions
Exercise 18

A Major Triad Root Position

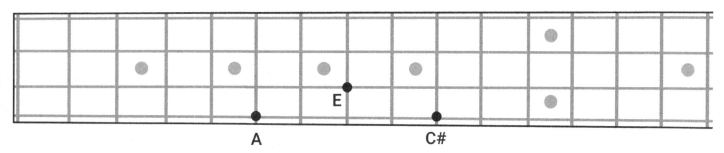

A Major Triad 1st Inversion

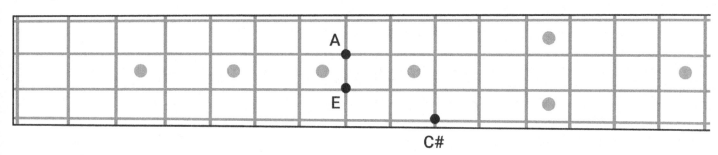

A Major Triad 2nd Inversion

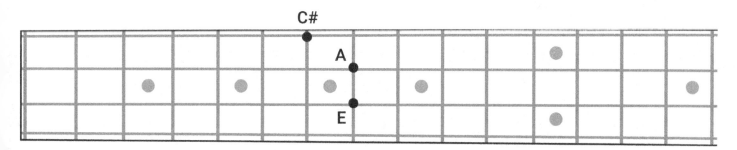

A Major Triad Root Position

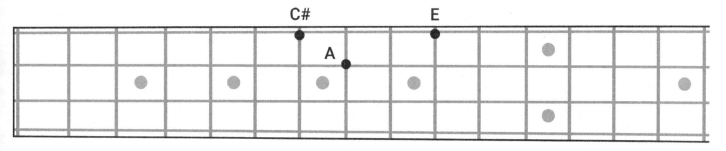

A Minor Triad Inversions
Exercise 19

Below is an example of what an A Minor Triad inversion looks like across the fretboard.

A Minor Triad Root Position

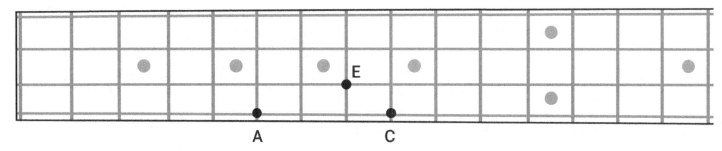

A Minor Triad 1st Inversion

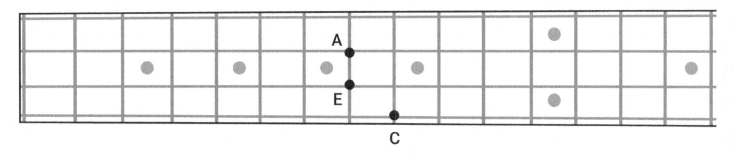

A Minor Triad 2nd Inversion

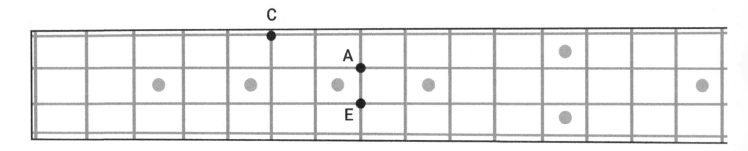

A Minor Triad Root Position

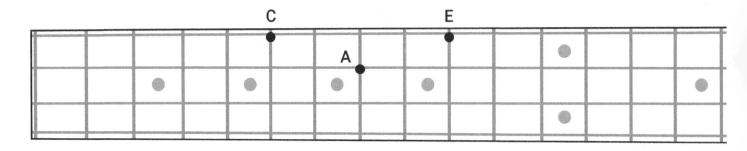

Below is an example of what an A Diminished Triad inversion looks like across the fretboard.

A Diminished Triad
Exercise 20

A Diminished Triad Root Position

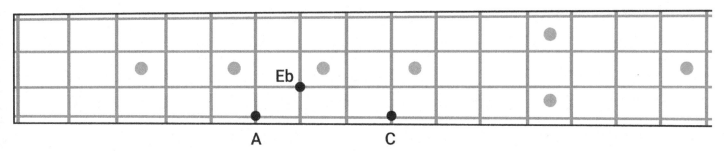

A Diminished Triad 1st Inversion

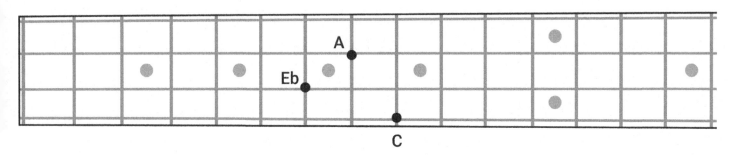

A Diminished Triad 2nd Inversion

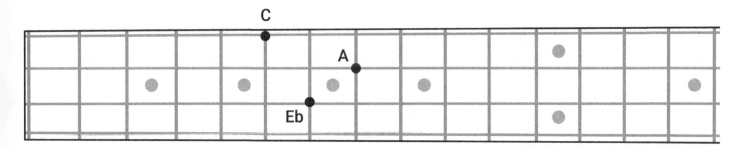

A Diminished Triad Root Position

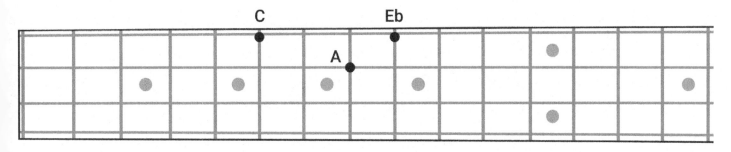

Below is an example of what an A Augmented Triad inversion looks like across the fretboard.

A Augmented Triad Inversion

Exercise 21

A Augmented Root Position

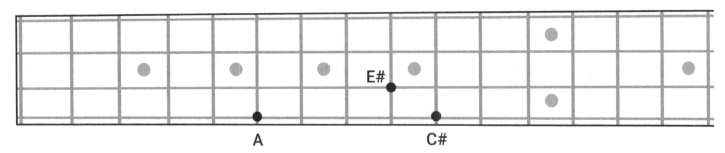

A Augmented 1st Inversion

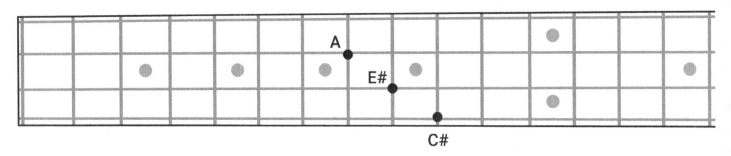

A Augmented 2nd Inversion

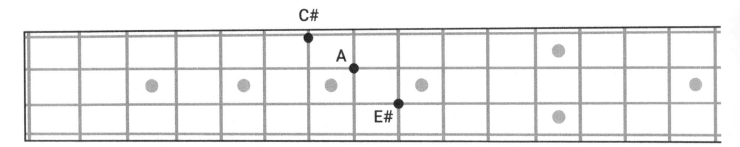

A Augmented Triad Root Position

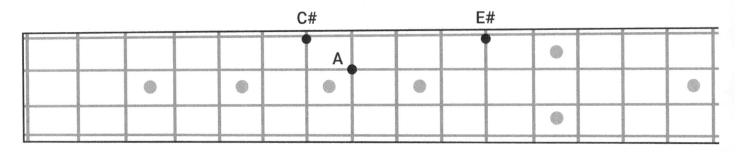

7ᵀᴴ CHORDS

7th chords are simply triads with the 7th note of the scale added on top. So, for example if we add a major 7th interval to a major triad, the triad turns into a Major 7th chord.

If we follow this principle for all 4 triad types, it gives us the following 4 note chords.

MAJOR 7

The notes of the Major 7 chord are A, C#, E, G#

A Major 7

Exercise 22

A Major 7 – Across 1 String

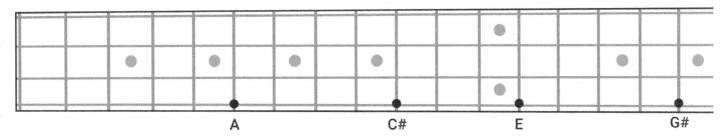

A Major 7 – Across 2 Strings

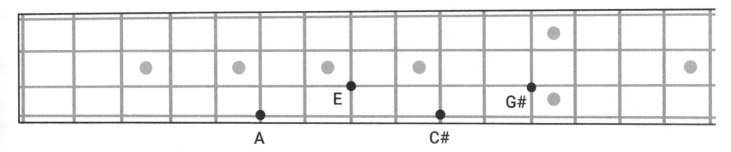

A Major 7 – Across 3 Strings

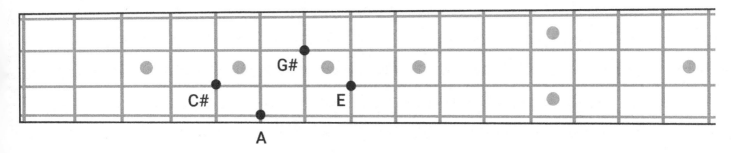

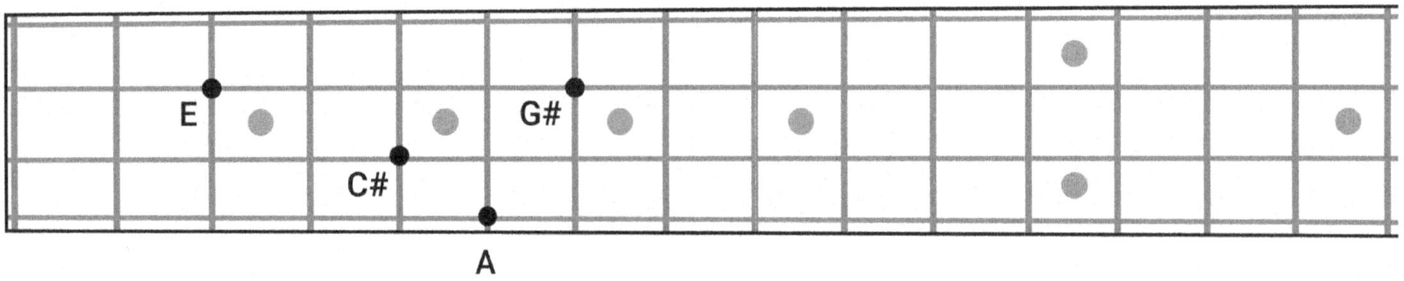
E
G#
C#
A

MINOR 7

The notes of the Minor 7 chord are A, C, E, G

A Minor 7
Exercise 23

A Minor 7 – Across 1 String

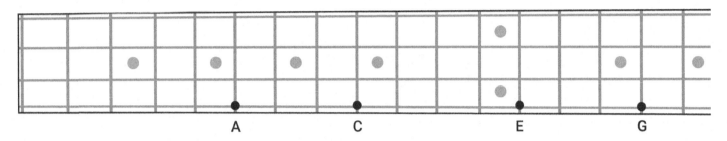

A Minor 7 – Across 2 Strings

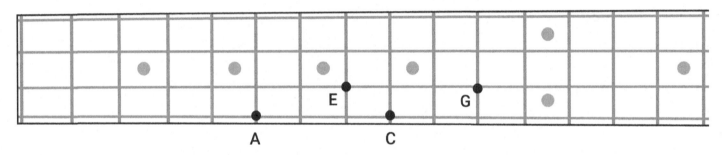

A Minor 7 – Across 3 Strings

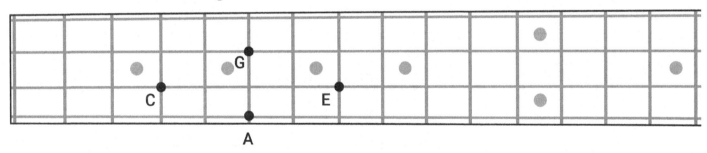

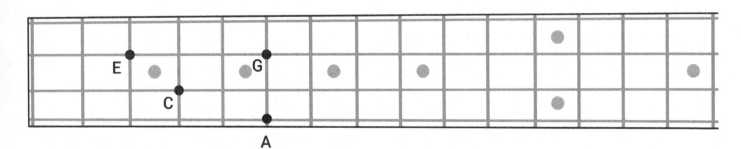

HALF-DIMINISHED OR MINOR 7 ♭ 5

The notes of the Half-Diminished chord are A, C, E♭, G.

A Half- Diminished or Minor 7 ♭5
Exercise 24

A Half Diminished or Minor 7 ♭5 – Across 1 String

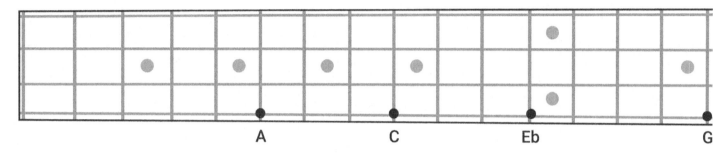

A Half Diminished or Minor 7 ♭5 – Across 2 Strings

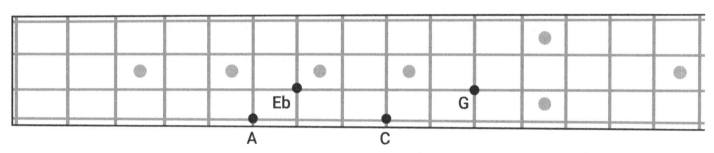

A Half Diminished or Minor 7 5♭ – Across 3 Strings

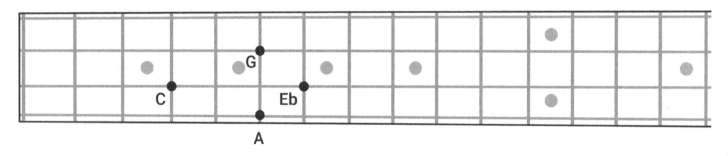

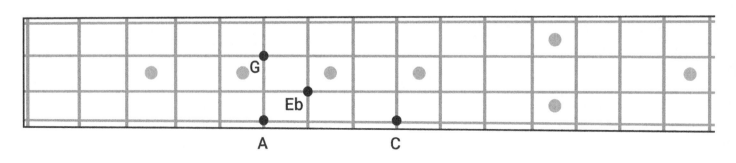

AUGMENTED 7

The notes of the Augmented 7 chord are A, C#, E#, G#

Augmented 7
Exercise 25

A Augmented 7 – Across 1 String

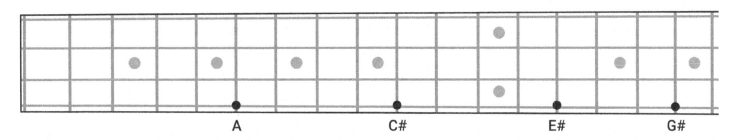

A Augmented 7 – Across 2 Strings

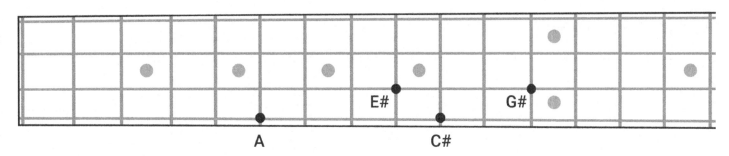

A Augmented 7 – Across 3 Strings

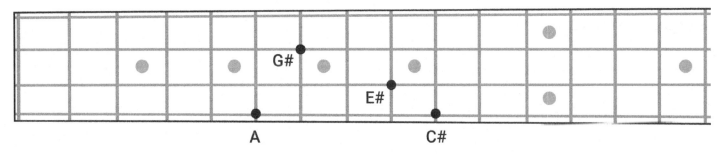

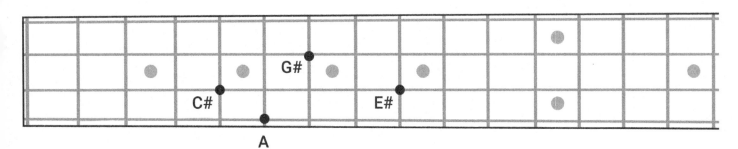

7TH CHORD INVERSIONS

Let's look at the chords with their inversions. Below is an example of what an A Major 7 inversion looks like across the fretboard. Again, take the time to work out the inversions using all the string options.

Exercise 26

A Major 7 Root Position

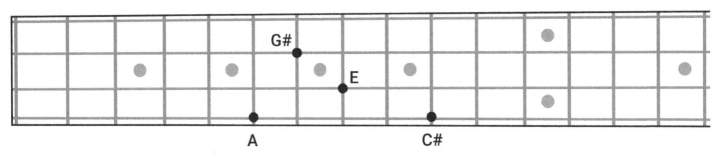

A Major 7 1st Inversion

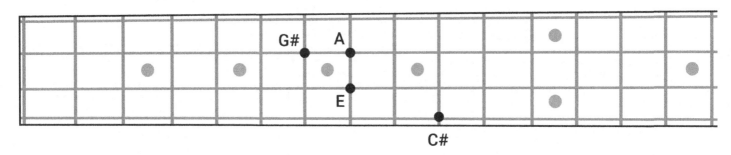

A Major 7 2nd Inversion

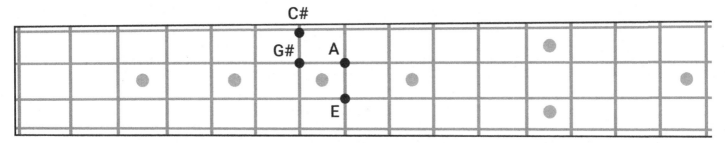

A Major 7 3rd Inversion

Below is an example of what the A Minor 7 inversions looks like across the fretboard.

Exercise 27

A Minor 7 Root Position

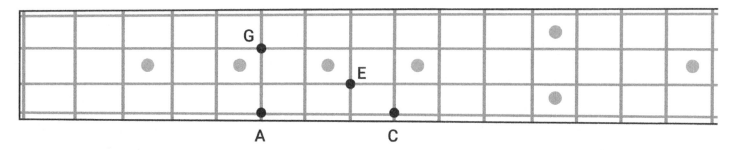

A Minor 7 1st Inversion

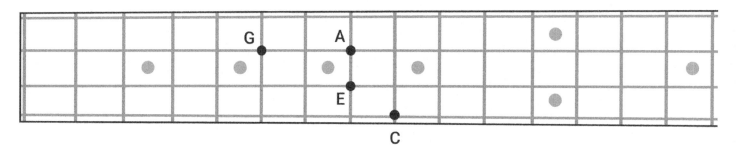

A Minor 7 2nd Inversion

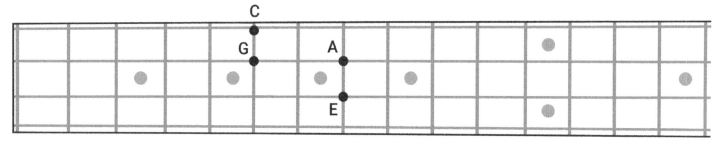

A Minor 7 3rd Inversion

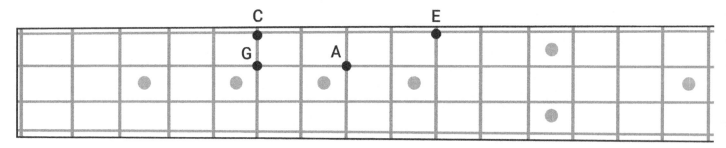

Below is an example of what the A Half Diminished inversions looks like across the fretboard.

Exercise 28

A Half Diminished Root Position

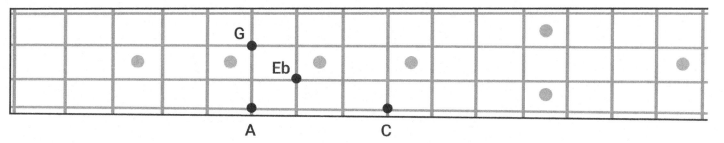

A Half Diminished 1st Inversion

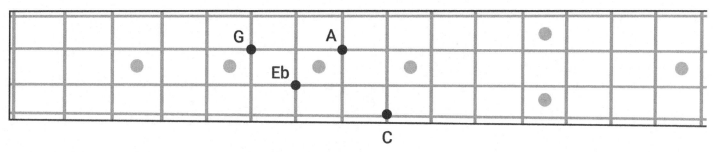

A Half Diminished 2nd Inversion

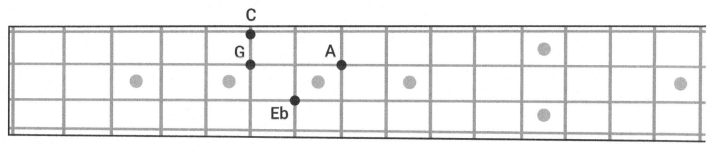

A Half Diminished 3rd Inversion

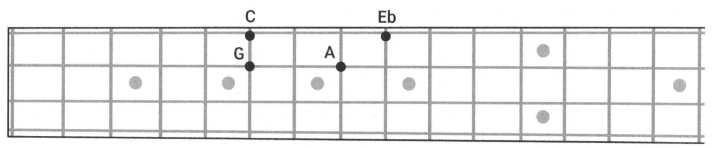

Below is an example of what an A Augmented 7 inversion looks like across the fretboard.

Exercise 29

A Augmented 7 Root Position

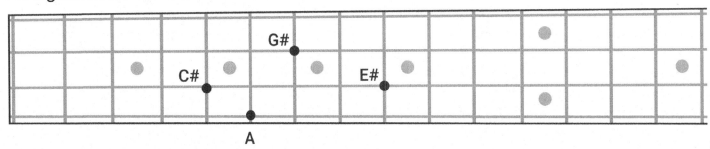

A Augmented 7 1st Inversion

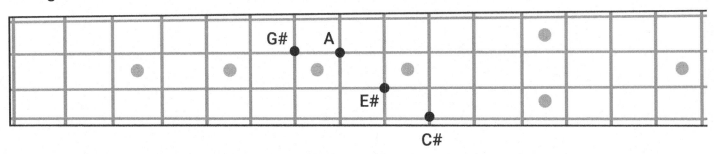

A Augmented 7 2nd Inversion

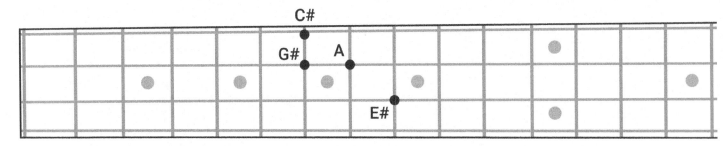

A Augmented 7 3rd Inversion

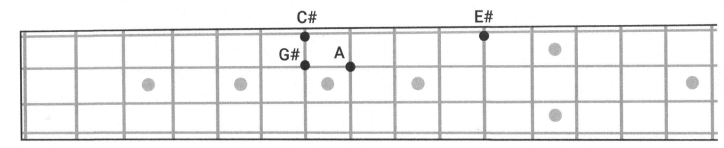

~ PART 7 ~
HARMONIZING THE MAJOR SCALE

HARMONIZING THE MAJOR SCALE SHAPES

In music, every scale can be harmonized, meaning chords and triads can be derived from any note within any scale.

(This means at every degree of the scale we can expand on that note and create harmony.)

This is important to learn as it provides the foundation that helps us understand and identify chords within the scale. It also helps us begin to see how chord progressions work within music.

In Part 6, we spent some time looking at triads and 7th chords. Now that we are familiar with these chords types, let's look at the formula that tells us which triad or chord type is assigned to each degree of the scale.

If you remember, a major triad is built up of the 1st, 3rd and 5th note of the major scale. Using the major scale, if we follow this principle, by selecting every other note in the scale we can work out the chord or harmony of that particular note. Let's continue to use the A major scale as an example.

A - B - C# - D - E - F# - G# - A

The 1st, 3rd and 5th note of the scale gives us our first triad of an A Major. Let's work out the triad for the next note in the scale, note B.

Starting on note B, if we select every other note until we have our 3 triad notes, this will give us B, D and F#: a B Minor triad. Therefore, the 2nd note of the major scale harmonizes to a minor chord.

If we follow this principle, we will be able to determine the chord type (harmony) for each degree of the scale.

The following table outlines the chord qualities for each degree of the major scale.

SCALE DEGREE	TRIADS	7TH CHORDS
1st	Major	Major 7
2nd	Minor	Minor 7
3rd	Minor	Minor 7
4th	Major	Major 7
5th	Major	Dominant 7
6th	Minor	Minor 7
7th	Diminished	Half Diminished

Exercise 30

Using the fretboard diagrams on the next page as a guide, play through the major scale using the triads. Start each triad on the E string, meaning your starting point will be E string, fret 5 (note A). The next triad will start on fret 7 on E string, (note B) and so on.

Begin with triads only first.

Exercise 31

When you feel comfortable harmonizing the major scale with triads, add the 7th note to the exercise.

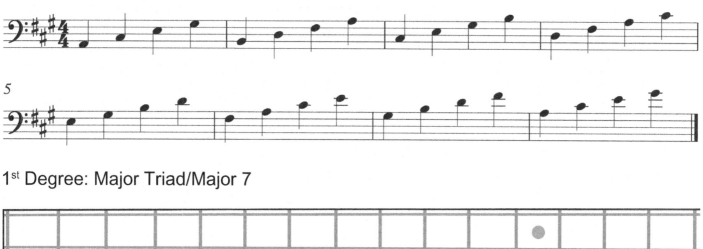

1st Degree: Major Triad/Major 7

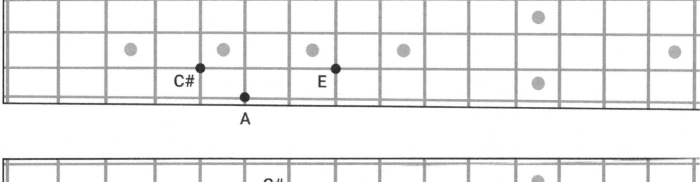

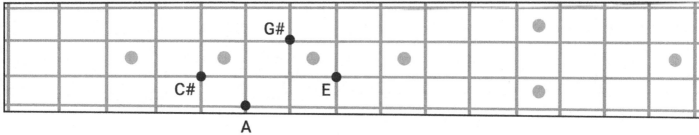

2nd Degree: Minor Triad/Minor 7

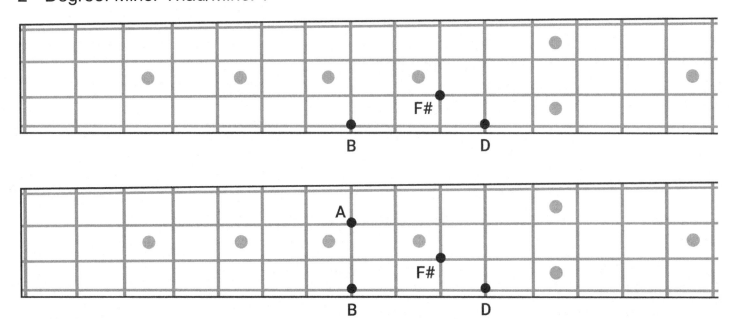

3rd Degree: Minor Triad/Minor 7

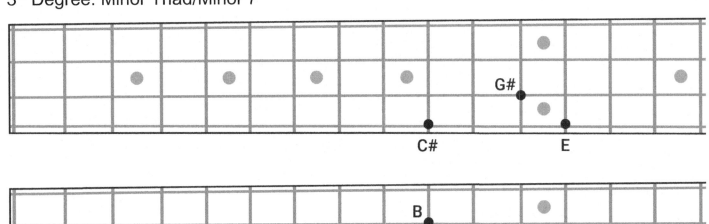

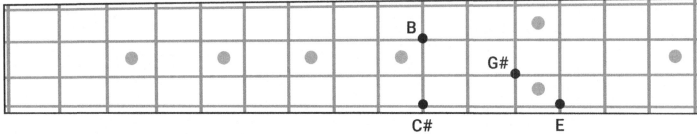

4th Degree: Major Triad/Major 7

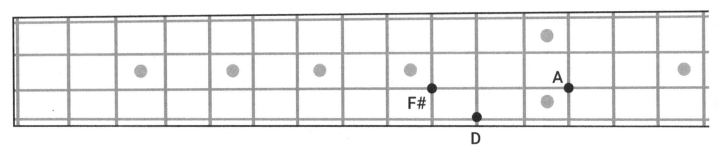

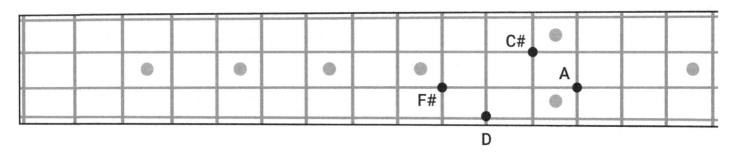

5th Degree: Major/Dom 7

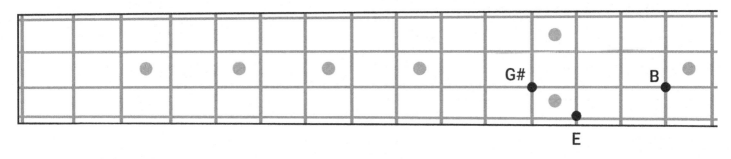

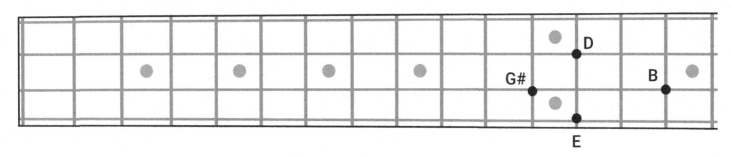

6th Degree: Minor/Minor 7

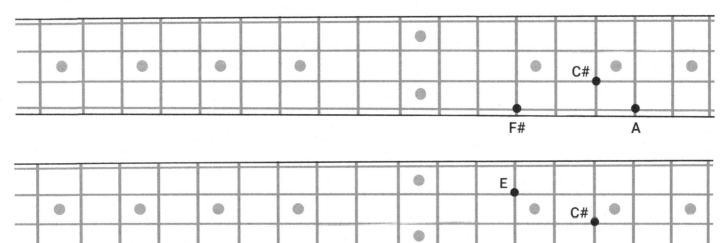

7th Degree: Diminished/Half Diminished

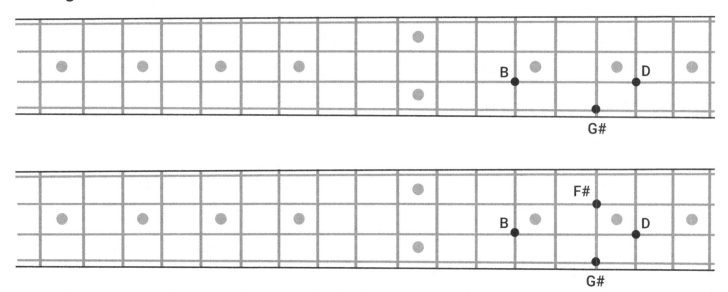

Exercise 32

This time, play through the exercise using the major scale 3 string position shape as your starting point. Again, start by using triads only.

Exercise 33

When you feel comfortable, add the 7th note to the exercise.

HARMONIZING THE MAJOR SCALE - EXTENSIONS

At this stage it's important to include the chord extensions when looking at harmonizing the major scale.

In the same way, we can add those extensions to build on the chord harmony when harmonizing the major scale.

The fretboard diagrams below will outline what those extensions look like in relation to the root note of each scale chord. I have left out the 1st, 3rd, 5th and 7th note so that you can more clearly see the shape of the extensions.

It is important to remember that every note must fall within the scale, therefore we will often have a flat ' ♭ ' or sharp ' # ' added to the extension in order to adhere to this rule.

For example, in the key of 'A': in the 4th chord of the scale, our note extension of an '11' will be amended to a '#11'. This is because we know that an 11th interval is the distance of 17 semitones from the root note of a chord, however, 17 intervals up from the root note of the 4th chord, D Major 7, will land us on note G.

As note G is not within the A major scale, we will need to amend the note to the nearest available note within the scale, which is G#. We would not use the F# as, from the 4th chord, D Major 7, F# has already been assigned the interval of a major 10th.

Since G# is now 18 semitones away from the root note of our 4th chord D Major 7, that changes the interval from an 11th to an Augmented or #11.

If necessary, refer back to Part 5 and 6 of the book to ensure you clearly understand the principles of intervals and chord building before moving forward with this section of the book.

1st Degree: A (Major) - 9, 11, 13

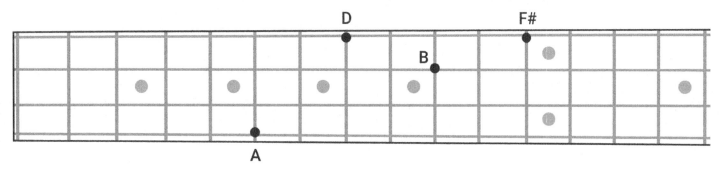

2nd Degree: B (Minor) - 9, 11, 13

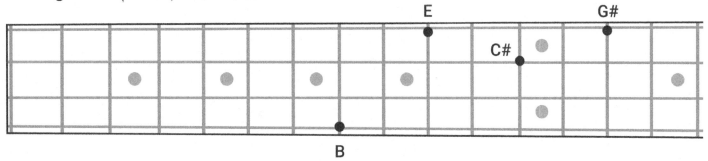

3rd Degree: C# (Minor) - b9, 11, b13

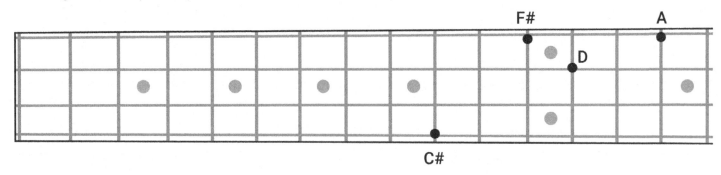

4th Degree: D (Major) - 9, #11, 13

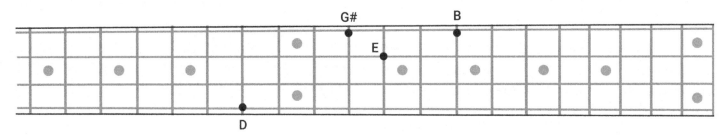

5th Degree: E (Major) - 9, 11, 13

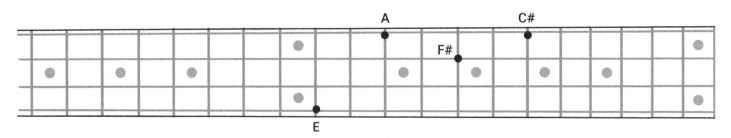

6th Degree: F# (Minor) - 9, 11, b13

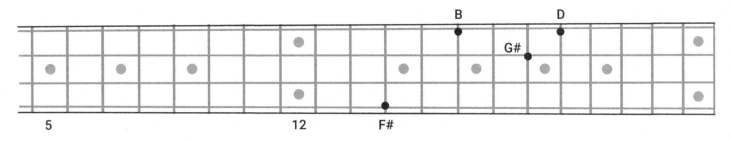

7th Degree: G# (Diminished) - b9, 11, b13

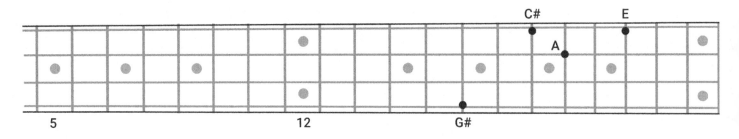

Chord extension studies go much further than what I have included in this book, but there are a lot of resources available if you want to study this further.

~ PART 8 ~
CIRCLE OF FIFTHS

CIRCLE OF FIFTHS

The circle of fifths is a system used in music theory to describe the connection between all 12 chromatic notes. It's a great way to determine the key signatures of the 12 major keys and the 12 minor keys.

A key signature refers to the number of sharps or flats that belong to any given major scale. You will remember that we covered the notes of the 12 major scales in Part 3 of the book. Here, we discovered that there are a certain number of sharps # or flats ♭ that belong to each scale.

It also helps determine the relative 12 minor keys of each major scale. We will look more at the natural minor scale in part 9 of this book, but for now, let's take a look at how the circle of fifths works.

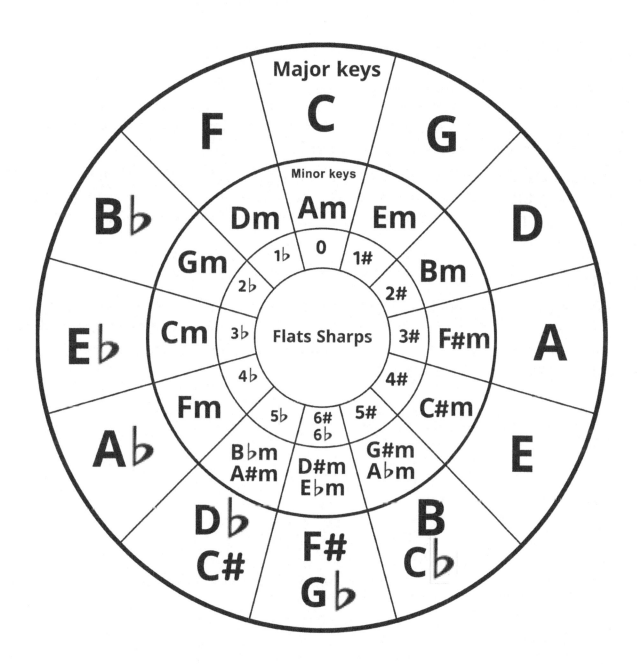

HOW IT WORKS

As you can see, the diagram moves in steps of a Perfect 5th interval when going clockwise and in steps of a Perfect 4th interval moving counter- clockwise.

The outer layer of the circle represents the 12 major keys, whilst the middle layer represents each major key's relative minor key.

RELATIVE MINOR KEYS

The relative minor key is the key or scale that shares the same notes as its associated major scale. The inner layer tells us how many sharp and flat notes occur in each key. As you can see, the major key and its relative minor will share the same sharp and flat notes.

FINDING PRIMARY CHORDS

Chords 1, 4 and 5 are defined as Primary Chords. If you select any key, for chord 1 and move one step counter-clockwise, that gives us chord 4. If we move 1 step clockwise from chord 1, that gives us chord 5. So in the key of C, to the left (counter-clockwise) we have our F (chord 4). To the right of C (clockwise) we have our G (chord 5).

There are a lot more concepts that can be pulled from looking at the circle of 5ths, like identifying cadences, finding 3rds and much more. In this book, we are just going to look at the basic foundational functions of the circle of fifths but it is certainly worth exploring this further on your own time.

Study Tip ☀

As bass players, our instrument is tuned in Perfect 4th intervals. One great way for us to practice scales, triads and any of these exercises is to move them around in 4ths until we work our way through all 12 chromatic notes. Try implementing that into your practice as a way of becoming comfortable with moving around the fretboard.

~ PART 9 ~
THE NATURAL MINOR SCALE

THE NATURAL MINOR SCALE

There are 3 main minor scales. The natural minor, the harmonic minor and the melodic minor. In their simplest form, the differences between the 3 minor scales are as follows.

The natural minor scale is built similarly and contains most of the same intervals as the major scale, but has the following fundamental differences. Instead of a major 3rd, 6th and 7th, we have a minor 3rd, minor 6th and minor 7th interval.

The Harmonic Minor scale contains a minor 3rd and minor 6th, but this time we raise minor 7th by a semitone to give us a major 7th.

The Melodic Minor scale contains a minor 3rd, but this time we raise the minor 6th to a major 6th and we retain the major 7th. In classical music, both the major 6th and major 7th intervals are flattened to a minor 6th and minor 7th interval when playing the scale descending.

In this section, we will concentrate on the natural minor scale only.

As mentioned in the circle of fifths section of this book, the relative minor is the key or scale that shares the same notes with its associated major key or scale. If necessary, refer back to the circle of fifths diagram as a point of reference.

The natural minor scale is taken directly from the major scale, so beginning of the 6th degree of the C major scale, note A, walk through the major scale until we arrive back at note A.

Doing this will give us the notes of the natural minor scale. It is essentially the same scale, but instead, we are moving through the notes of the scale from a different starting point and therefore have a different ending point.

This principle is known as 'modal playing' or 'modes'. Remember this concept as it will be vital when we begin to develop scale knowledge. Let's use the C major scale as an example.

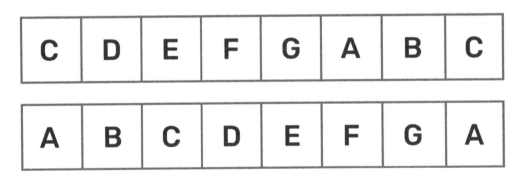

The formula or steps of the Minor scale will be as follows.

Tone Semitone Tone Tone Semitone Tone Tone, or often written in short as T S T T S T T.

Just as with the major scale, we should never mix sharps and flats in the same key and we never repeat the same letter name twice when writing the scale.

MINOR SCALE SHAPES ACROSS THE FRETBOARD

Here are the shapes for the natural minor scale. As with the major scale I have demonstrated them across 1, 2, 3 & 4 strings and two octaves. Again, I have included a table that will give you a 'fingering guide' to use when playing through these scale patterns.

The number below each note is the finger you should be using to play that particular note. Use your 1st finger to play the scale across 1 string.

Exercise 34

A Minor Scale - Across 1 String

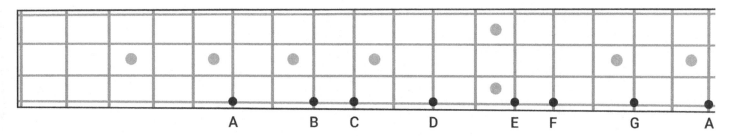

Exercise 35 - A Minor Scale - Across 2 Strings

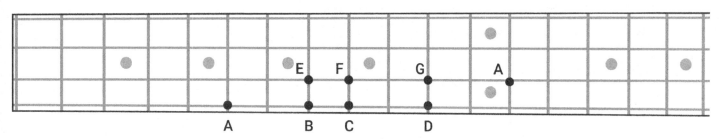

Fingering Table

A	B	C	D	E	F	G	A
1	1	2	4	1	2	4	4

Exercise 36 - A Minor Scale - Across 3 Strings

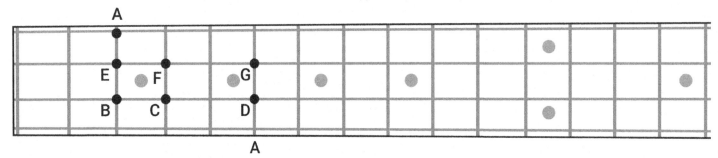

A	B	C	D	E	F	G	A
1	3	4	1	3	4	1	3

Exercise 37 - A Minor Scale - Across 4 Strings

A	B	C	D	E	F	G	A
4	1	2	4	1	2	4	1

Exercise 38 - A Minor Scale - Across Two Octaves

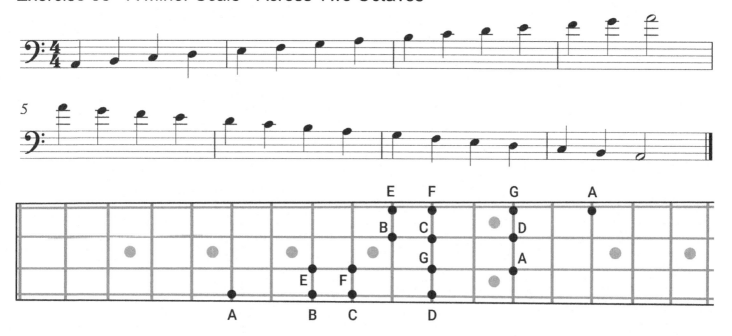

1st Octave

A	B	C	D	E	F	A
1	1	2	4	1	2	4

2nd Octave

A	B	C	D	E	F	G	A
4	1	2	4	1	2	4	4

Study Tip! 💡

As with the major scale, there are many ways you can play the minor scale over two octaves. Using the examples you have been shown, see how many other ways you can play this scale over two octaves. In all examples, learn to play the scale in both ascending and descending ways.

Remember to play them with a metronome and challenge yourself to play it at higher speeds moving up in increments of 10 bpm.

~ PART 10 ~
THE PENTATONIC SCALE

THE MAJOR PENTATONIC SCALE

Along with the major scale, the pentatonic is one of the most commonly used scales in modern western music. The scale is derived from the major scale and only contains 5 notes, hence its name 'Penta' meaning 5 and 'tonic' meaning tones.

These 5 notes are the 1st, 2nd, 3rd, 5th and 6th degrees of the major scale, giving us the following intervals:

Root, Major 2nd, Major 3rd, Perfect 5th, and Major 6th.

In the Key of A, these are the notes of the A major pentatonic scale. A B C# E F# A.

Since we are already familiar with the major scale and how it is built up, let's go ahead and learn what the pentatonic shape looks like across the fretboard. As with each scale, start by learning what the shape looks like across 1 & 2 strings before moving on to the 3 string positions. We will use the key of A to demonstrate the shapes across the fretboard.

Exercise 39

Play the following scale using your first finger.

A Major Pentatonic - Across 1 string

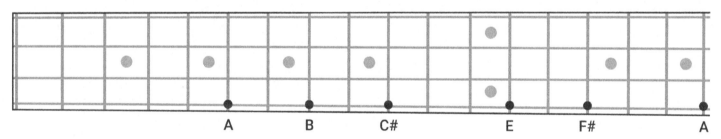

Exercise 40 - A Major Pentatonic - Across 2 strings

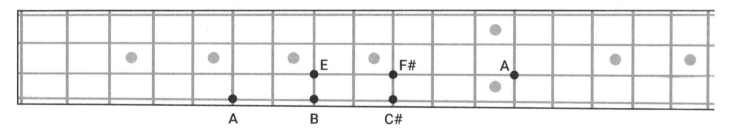

Fingering Table

A	B	C#	E	F#	A
1	1	4	1	4	4

Exercise 41 - A Major Pentatonic - Across 3 strings

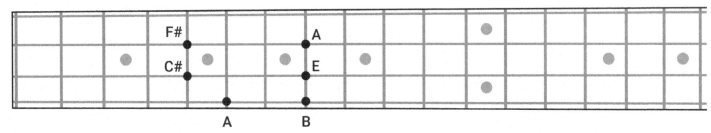

A	B	C#	E	F#	A
2	4	1	4	1	4

Option 2

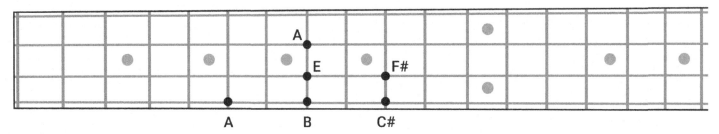

A	B	C#	E	F#	A
1	1	4	1	4	1

Exercise 42 - A Major Pentatonic - Two Octaves

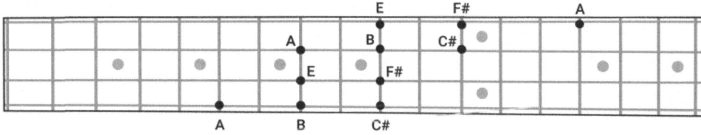

1st Octave

A	B	C#	E	F#
1	1	4	1	4

2nd Octave

A	B	C#	E	F#	A
1	1	4	1	1	4

Study Tip!

As with the previous scales we have covered, see how many other ways you can play this scale over two octaves.

In all examples, learn to play the scale both ascending and descending.

Remember to play them with a metronome and challenge yourself to play them at higher speeds.

THE MINOR PENTATONIC SCALE

As with the major scale, the major pentatonic scale also has its associated relative minor pentatonic scale. If you recall, the natural minor scale begins and ends on the 6th degree of the major scale. We derive the minor pentatonic scale in the same way. In the key of A Major, F# would be the 5th note in the major pentatonic scale. If we play the 5 notes of the major pentatonic scale, beginning on note F# and playing through to note F#, we are playing the notes of the F# minor pentatonic scale.

Let's take a look at the minor pentatonic shapes across the fretboard.

Exercise 43

Play the following scale using your first finger.

F# Minor Pentatonic - Across 1 string

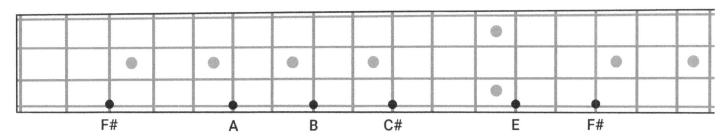

Exercise 44 - F# Minor Pentatonic - Across 2 Strings

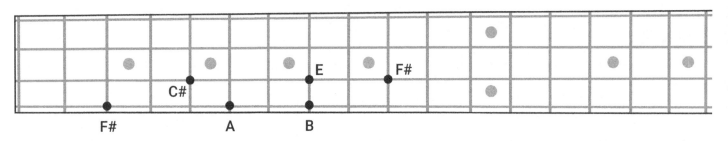

F#	A	B	C#	E	F#
1	4	4	1	4	4

Exercise 45 - F# Minor Pentatonic - Across 3 Strings

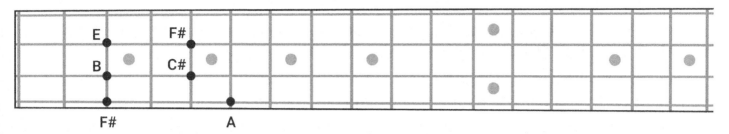

Fingering Table

F#	A	B	C#	E	F#
1	4	1	3	1	3

Exercise 46 - F# Minor Pentatonic – Two Octaves

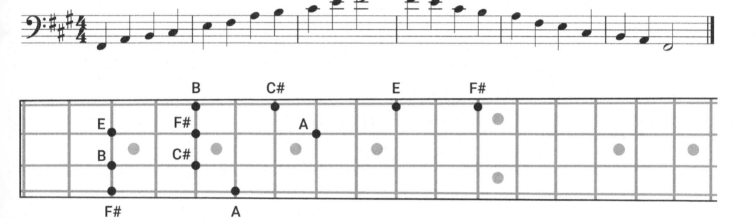

1st Octave

F#	A	B	C#	E
1	4	1	3	1

2nd Octave

F#	A	B	C#	E	F#
4	4	1	1	4	4

THE 5 PENTATONIC POSITIONS

Earlier in the book, we looked very briefly at the definition of modes. The 5 positions of the pentatonic scale work in exactly the same way.

Starting from each point of the major pentatonic scale and using the concept of modes we will learn what each shape looks like across the fretboard.

Learning to play the pentatonic scales in all 5 positions gives us the tools we need to move up and down the fretboard with more freedom.

This time, when playing the scale, keep playing all the notes in each position to cover all 4 strings. This CAGED system of playing all available notes in the scales gives us the ability to achieve more freedom across the fretboard.

A Major Pentatonic Scale in 5 Positions

Exercise 47

1st Position

2nd Position

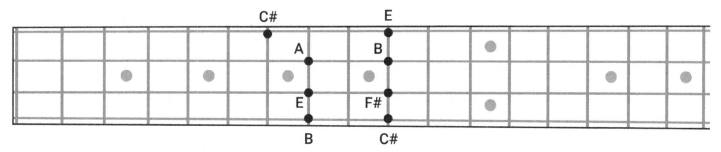

3rd Position

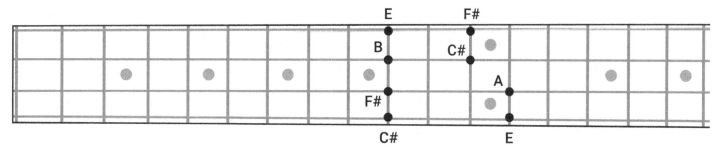

4th Position

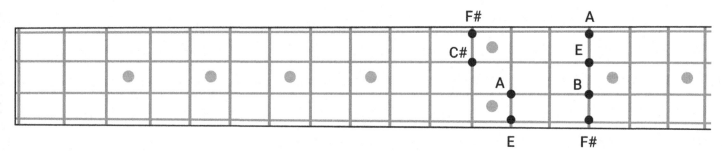

5th Position

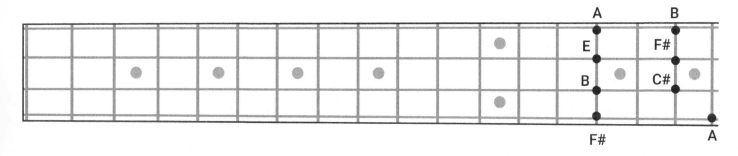

1st Position

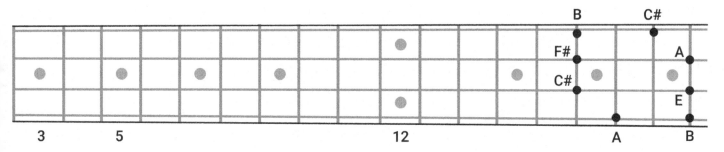

Study Tip!

Again, just like the previous exercises, learn to play the scale both ascending and descending.

Try playing the scale ascending in position 1, then descending in position 2 and so on through all 5 positions. Explore all the options available to you.

Once you are comfortable with playing the 5 positions in this key, begin to move through all 12 keys using the system of perfect 4ths.

Remember to always practice these exercises with a metronome and challenge yourself to play them at higher speeds.

~ APPENDIX ~

Song 1

(Rock Pop)   Triads - Practice Song 1

$\frac{4}{4}$|C$_\Delta$ |G$_\Delta$ |A– |F$_\Delta$ |

|C$_\Delta$ |G$_\Delta$ |F$_\Delta$ |F$_\Delta$ |

|C$_\Delta$ |G$_\Delta$ |F$_\Delta$ |A– |

|C$_\Delta$ |G$_\Delta$ |D– |G$_\Delta$ ‖

Song 2

(Rock Pop)   Triads - Practice Song 2

$\frac{4}{4}$|G$_\Delta$ |D$_\Delta$ |E– |B– |

|C$_\Delta$ |B– |C$_\Delta$ |D$_\Delta$ |

|G$_\Delta$ |D$_\Delta$ |E– |B– |

|C$_\Delta$ |B– |C$_\Delta$ |D$_\Delta$ ‖

Song 3

(Reggae)   Triads - Practice Song 3

$\frac{4}{4}$ | D_Δ | D_Δ | D_Δ | D_Δ |

| G_Δ | G_Δ | D_Δ | D_Δ |

| A_Δ | G_Δ | D_Δ | A_Δ ‖

Song 4

(Reggae)   Triads - Practice Song 4

$\frac{4}{4}$ ‖: A_Δ | A_Δ | B_Δ | $C^{\#}_-$ |

| A_Δ | A_Δ | B_Δ | $C^{\#}_-$:‖

Song 5

(Pop)   Practice Song 5

$\frac{4}{4}$ ‖: A△ | D△ | B- | E△ |
| A/C♯ | F♯- | B- | E△ :‖

Song 6

(Medium Swing)   7th Chords - Practice Song 6

$\frac{4}{4}$ | F7 | B♭7 | F7 | C- F7 |
| B♭7 | B♭7 | A-7 | D7 |
| G7 | C7 | F7 D7 | G7 C7 ‖

Song 7

(Medium Swing) 7th Chords - Practice Song 7

$\frac{4}{4}$ | B^b_7 | E^b_7 | B^b_7 | F_{-7} B^b_7 |

| E^b_7 | E^b_7 | B^b_7 | G_7 |

| C_{-7} | F_7 | B^b_7 | F_7 ‖

Song 8

(RnB) 7th Chords - Practice Song 8

$\frac{4}{4}$ | $F_{\Delta7}$ | A_{-7} G | $F_{\Delta7}$ | A_{-7} G_7 |

| D_{-7} | A_{-7} G | D_{-7} | $B^b_{\Delta7}$ G_Δ ‖

ABOUT THE AUTHOR

British Bassist Michelle Marie Osbourne, now based in the U.S, has had the privilege to work and travel with some prominent artists and producers alike. Born and raised in London, England, Michelle's musical journey started in her late teens. Michelle studied at the BRIT Performing Arts and Technology school & The Institute of Contemporary Music Performance (formerly known as the Guitar Institute and Bass Tech).

During her time of study, Michelle met and worked with some of the UK's most established musicians, artists and songwriters.

To date, Michelle has been afforded the opportunity to work with artists including Gloria Gaynor, Jessie J, Emeli Sande, and Jocelyn Brown to name a few. In addition to working with recording artists, Michelle is also involved in New York's theatre scene and has worked on various theatre projects and showcases including off-Broadway show 'Black Light' and new Broadway show 'SIX' The Musical. Michelle continues to work and teach within NYC's thriving music scene.

Made in the USA
Columbia, SC
14 February 2022

56185531R10063